INSPIRATIONAL GUIDE FOR THE IMPLEMENTATION OF PRME

UK and Ireland Edition

PRₘE Principles for Responsible
Management Education

CHAPTER
UK AND IRELAND

Greenleaf
PUBLISHING

PRME Principles for Responsible
Management Education
CHAPTER
UK AND IRELAND

First published 2015

By Greenleaf Publishing Ltd
Aizlewood's Mill
Nursery Street
Sheffield S3 8GG
UK
www.greenleaf-publishing.com

Typeset by OKS
Printed and bound by CPI Group (UK) Ltd, Croydon, CR0 4YY

Cataloguing in Publication data:
   A catalogue record for this book is available from the British Library.

ISBN -13: 978-1-783531-25-7 [hardback]
ISBN -13: 978-1-783531-24-0 [paperback]
ISBN -13: 978-1-783531-26-4 [PDF eBook]
ISBN -13: 978-1-783531-27-1 [ePub eBook]

Contents

Part C – Developing programmes in research and learning and teaching 83

Foreword

As the Principles for Responsible Management Education (PRME) initiative comes into its 8th year, the movement is developing more and more into a network of networks—individuals, institutions and communities collaborating on both global and regional levels, with a number of activities that support the implementation of this UN-supported initiative. The launch of PRME regional Chapters gives further evidence to this development; within only two years since their initiation in 2012, ten regional PRME Chapters have emerged around the world. Decided together as a group, each PRME Chapter has its priority areas and activities for addressing responsible management education in the region. These regional platforms ground PRME in the different national, regional, cultural and linguistic contexts, facilitating the growth and engagement of responsible management education, and serve as prime examples of the dedication at many levels to fostering responsible, sustainability-aware future leaders through higher education.

This PRME *Inspirational Guide* for UK and Ireland is a direct outcome of the discussions from the regional PRME Chapter UK and Ireland. With examples coming from academic institutions across the region, drawing connections to the local community, business, the classroom, and covering the Six Principles of PRME—purpose, values, method, research, partnership and dialogue—it will be a precious resource for the practitioners and implementers of PRME not only in the region, but also around the globe.

Jonas Haertle, Head, PRME Secretariat,
UN Global Compact

PRME Principles for Responsible Management Education

**Greenleaf Publishing/PRME Book Series –
For Responsibility in Management Education**

The Greenleaf Publishing/Principles for Responsible Management Education (PRME) book series aims to highlight the important work of PRME, a United Nations supported initiative. The series will provide tools and inspiration for all those working to make management education fit for purpose in creating a new generation of enlightened leaders for the 21st century.

Acknowledgements

Co-editors:

Alan Murray
Denise Baden
Paul Cashian
Alec Wersun
Kathryn Haynes

Commissioned by the regional PRME Chapter UK and Ireland Secretariat.

The editors would like to thank the PRME Secretariat for their help and encouragement with this publication. We would also like to thank Rebecca Macklin at Greenleaf for her guidance and gentle encouragement as we compiled this volume.

Higher education institutions submitted case studies for the UK and Ireland edition of the *Inspirational Guide* in response to an open call for contributions to the 2014 PRME UK and Ireland Chapter Regional First Summit and were selected through a blind review process.

Disclaimer

The PRME UK and Ireland Secretariat makes no representation concerning, and does not guarantee, the source, originality, accuracy, completeness, or reliability of any statement, information, data, finding, interpretation, advice, or opinion contained within this publication.

This publication is intended strictly as a learning document. The inclusion of examples does not in any way constitute an endorsement of the individual academic institution or organisation by the PRME Secretariat, or the regional PRME Chapter UK and Ireland Secretariat. The material in this publication may be quoted and used provided there is proper attribution.

About PRME

The Principles for Responsible Management Education (PRME) is a United Nations Global Compact sponsored initiative with the mission to inspire and champion responsible management education, research and thought leadership globally. The Six Principles of PRME are inspired by internationally accepted values, such as the Ten Principles of the Global Compact. They seek to establish a process of continuous improvement among institutions of management education in order to develop a new generation of business leaders capable of managing the complex challenges faced by business and society in the 21st century. Currently, over 500 signatories have signed up to PRME, representing 80 countries. PRME's Steering Committee comprises global and specialised associations, including AACSB International (the Association to Advance Collegiate Schools of Business), the European Foundation for Management Development (EFMD), the Association of MBAs (AMBA), the Graduate Management Admission Council (GMAC), the Association of African Business Schools (AABS), the Association of Asia–Pacific Business Schools (AAPBS), CEEMAN (formerly Central and East European Management Development Association), CLADEA (the Latin American Council of Management Schools), ABIS (The Academy of Business in Society, formerly EABIS), and the Globally

Responsible Leadership Initiative (GRLI). For more information, please visit www.unprme.org.

The Six Principles of PRME and the Ten Principles of the Global Compact can be viewed in full in Appendices 1 and 2.

How to use the Guide

Over 500 signatory institutions from around the world are working to transform the way they train the next generation of leaders and managers using the Principles for Responsible Management Education (PRME), both as a framework derived from universally accepted sustainability principles and as part of a dynamic learning community. The ways in which they choose to do this are unique to each institution, and the Inspirational Guide project is an encouraging example of all of the different ways that responsible management can be embedded into the purpose and values of higher education institutions (HEIs) as well as the way that they teach students, conduct research, and interact with stakeholders. At the same time, challenges faced in mainstreaming sustainability principles remain for all HEIs, regardless of how long they have been signatory to PRME, the size of their institution, or where they are located in the world.

Before reading any single case, it is important to remember that:

- **All of the Six Principles are interrelated and often insep-arable.** This is exemplified by the fact that each case story covers more than one. For example, a research project (Principle 4) focused on responsible leadership (Principle 2) started because of involvement with PRME (Principle 1), involved a partnership with a local company (Principle 5), and resulted in a conference that aims to educate both students (Principle 3) and the business community about the outcomes (Principle 6).
- **It does not matter whether you are just starting out or have been a signatory for many years.** The range of case stories offers insights and lessons learnt for implementers of all levels.
- **It does not matter where the institution is located or how big it is.** Examples presented can easily be shaped and moulded to fit your own institution, resources, and focus areas.
- Many of the highlighted projects were put in place using limited resources, either in terms of staff or money, or both. **Often, all you need is a group of committed indi-viduals to champion these efforts and get things started.**

What is in each case story?

The case stories focus on a particular programme, project, or activity that an institution has implemented around responsible management. Each short case story contains:

- An **introduction** to the contributing institution and the story highlighted
- An overview of the particular **challenge(s) faced** in rela-tion to mainstreaming responsible management
- An explanation of the **actions taken** in relation to the challenge(s) outlined

- Information about the **results** and/or **benefits** of the actions taken
- Some points regarding **the role of PRME/sustainability principles** in helping to inspire and/or carry out the activity

The following case stories can be used as a source of:

- **New ideas and inspiration for how you can implement sustainability principles on your campus:** The case stories cover a wide range of different ways to embed responsible management into teaching, research, partnerships, and the culture of an institution, many of which are quite innovative.
- **Advice for schools thinking of implementing something similar:** You may already have decided that you want to create a similar programme, and seeing how other signatories have approached their respective initiatives may help to structure your thinking and next steps.
- **Inspiration on how to further your current efforts:** You may already be undertaking a similar activity on campus, and seeing how other institutions have implemented their projects can help you to further develop or scale efforts up.

What topics are covered?

The case stories cover a wide range of topics relevant both to new signatories that are just starting out and to schools with more established programmes. This includes, but is not limited to:

- How to get started
- How to embed responsible management into:
  - Institutional culture
  - Curriculum
  - Research and publications

- How to create and work with networks and partnerships
- How to evaluate progress and report on achievements

Want more information about what PRME signatories are doing?

The PRME community offers many different ways to share case stories and learn from others, including:

- The Inspirational Guide project
- Sharing Information on Progress (SIP) reports
- The *PRiMEtime* blog
- PRME Annual Assemblies
- Regional PRME Chapters and Meetings
- Working Group activities and PRME projects
- Share your story via social media. You can engage with PRME on Twitter, Facebook, and LinkedIn.
- Reach out to PRMESecretariat@unprme.org or to fellow signatories directly

Introduction

**Alan Murray, Denise Baden, Paul Cashian,
Kathryn Haynes and Alec Wersun**

Where we came from

In the autumn of 2006 a 'Concept Paper' was issued from
the United Nations Global Compact office by Manual Escudeo. In
light of the impending global financial meltdown it proved to
show amazing foresight, envisioning a new model for business
schools: forward looking, with principles of operation based on
responsible attitudes towards corporate ethics, the environment and human rights, encompassing the spirit of the UN
Global Compact and the UN Millennium Development Goals. By
summer 2007, the Principles of Responsible Management Education had been established.

This coincided with the formation of the British Academy of
Management Special Interest Group in Corporate Social Responsibility, and members of that group along with others, soon realised
the synergies that existed between these initiatives and set about
organising a series of events to support the growing interest in
research and teaching in the broad area of CSR and sustainability,
and to promote membership of PRME.

Over the next years a series of seminars and mini-conferences
were organised with the aim of appealing to: 1) new signatories—
to make them aware of the support on offer in terms of curriculum

change, faculty engagement and material support; 2) existing signatories—to help maintain the momentum for change especially in the more conservative areas of finance and strategy, for example; and 3) those wanting to go further—to explore new research directions and collaborations and innovative teaching methods.

As interest in PRME gathered momentum (a meeting at Aston Business School in 2009 attracted 75 delegates from seven countries), so signatories in the UK and Ireland began to seek new ways to sustain interest in the initiative and to continue to elicit increasing membership. By the time the Global Forum at Rio + 20 was announced we had already made representation to the PRME office for some form of regional representation. At the Forum, regional Chapters were announced and the establishment of the regional Chapter for the UK and Ireland was set in train.

As of June 2014, 48 business schools in the UK and Ireland, out of a total number of around 110, have signed up to PRME, with representatives from institutions across the spectrum of old and new, top tier research and top tier teaching.

How have we compiled this Guide?

Following on from the success of the *Inspirational Guides* published by the PRME Secretariat, we wanted to mark the establishment of the UK and Ireland Chapter with a collection of stories of our own, convinced that we knew of sufficient inspirational activity that a regional edition would be viable. We planned that the first UK and Ireland Chapter Forum would give authors the first opportunity to present their ideas, and thereafter give time to prepare a case story for publication. We were delighted to receive 21 submissions and the variety of approaches taken reflects the creativity and innovation of faculty to embed aspects of PRME in their school activities.

Indeed, in this Guide there are ideas that all schools should examine and case stories that all schools can learn from. They may offer guidance and inspiration to emulate or improve on what is outlined, but we are confident that any dean who is unsure of the value that attaches to participation in PRME, will feel that the minimal investment involved in being a signatory could be swiftly and easily repaid by adopting some of the initiatives outlined in this volume. More than that, we urge deans of schools who have not contributed a story, and deans of schools that have not yet signed up to PRME to discuss these case stories with colleagues, so that our next edition reflects an even wider group of schools and activities to inspire us all.

The next few years is sure to create new challenges for business schools as we seek to engage an agenda increasingly influenced by evidence from the Intergovernmental Panel on Climate Change. As further evidence emerges through 2014, we can surely anticipate further calls for increasing regulation on the one hand, and new business models to be developed to deal with this and other environmental pressures, coming from business and policy-makers, on the other.

The 'post millennium development goals' agenda, outlined by the UN Global Compact in its publication *Architects for a Better World: Building the Post-2015 Business Engagement Architecture*, sets a challenge to business schools to engage with this agenda and show leadership in providing solutions by developing, first, research agendas that will inform business behaviour in the years and decades to come and, second, teaching agendas to equip our graduates to understand and respond to the challenges they will face. It is fortuitous that this impetus towards changing practice resonates so neatly with the impact agenda now permeating higher education and informing research assessment exercises.

What we have compiled in this volume is a combination of individual approaches to enhance the teaching and learning experience of students, group activity to examine specific issues and challenges, and some more strategic approaches to align school values or missions with PRME.

Our contributions

A. Examining the values and mission of the school

Chapters 1–3

Picking up on the theme introduced in the previous section, our first contribution from Davidson *et al.* (Chapter 1) highlights work done at Strathclyde Business School to 'educate responsible managers today for the global challenges of tomorrow' in line with its position as a leading business school with an international reputation for excellence in several fields. They outline how ethics and CSR have been introduced as key learning outcomes for their Management Development Programme, and detail the positive feedback received from students, faculty and industry partners.

This theme is continued by Haynes (Chapter 2) and Gibbon and Haynes (Chapter 3) as they look at the mission of Newcastle University Business School and discuss how the PRME agenda can be utilised to add value to all of its stakeholders. In Chapter 2, Haynes examines how research agendas on gender equality inform and promote a common vision of equality and respect, both locally and globally, through the PRME Gender Equality Working Group and its engagement with the UN Women's Empowerment Principles. In Chapter 3, Gibbon and Haynes broaden their focus to examine how PRME can help 'build excellence as an internationally recognised business school', aligning the school's vision and role as a 'civic university' with its commitment to PRME, and its engagement with key stakeholders.

B. Developing centres and outreach initiatives embedding the values of PRME

Chapters 4–10

Under this broad heading we highlight five examples of schools developing initiatives to either establish specific structures to engage with external stakeholders, or programmes to foster various forms of outreach and engagement. Kempster and Watton open this section with a discussion around the relaunch of the Lancaster Leadership Centre, attached to the Lancaster University Management School, and the role of PRME in shaping some of the themes to be pursued. Tadeka and Lamont (Chapter 5) discuss the approach of Bournemouth University Business School in engaging students in local charity or community projects. Blakeley (Chapter 6) explains the approach Winchester Business School adopted to obtain support for its Centre for Responsible Management, and in Chapter 7, Lever *et al.* explore the evolution of the University of Huddersfield Business School's Centre for Sustainable and Resilient Communities, consolidating a sequence of events that began in 1994. In a similar vein, Hynes *et al.*, in Chapter 8, examine how, faced with 'a series of interlocking social and economic problems' in Limerick, Ireland, the Kemmy School of Business, University of Limerick developed two target initiatives: the establishment of a Centre for Academic Achievement, and the development of its Innovation, Creativity and Entrepreneurship programme.

In Chapter 9, Wersun *et al.* explain the approach taken by Glasgow Caledonian University in tackling the issue of widening access to higher education by the establishment of the 'Caledonian Club', working with five Glasgow communities with 'traditionally low levels of onward transition from school to higher education'. In Chapter 10, rounding off this section, Filosof discusses the initiatives adopted at Hertfordshire Business School to engage students with the local community through experiential learning and innovative learning and teaching strategies.

C. Developing programmes in research and learning and teaching

Chapters 11–23

In this section authors reflect on the development of lectures, modules, courses and programmes of study, embedding PRME through their curricula to develop graduate leaders equipped to understand the challenges ahead. In Chapter 11, Bass explains the influences that have shaped her approach at Coventry University Business School to module development, and in particular, out-lines the significance of discourse analysis in her teaching. Outlin-ing how Bradford University School of Management approached the Education for Sustainable Development project is the topic of Fukukawa's essay in Chapter 12, and her discussion of the change processes offers some useful insights. Baden broadens the discus-sion in Chapter 13 to discuss a particular research project under-taken at the School of Management, University of Southampton, working with a number of SMEs using action research to develop interventions in addressing sustainability issues. In Chapter 14, McLaughlin and Prothero return to the effects that the financial meltdown of 2008/9 had in Ireland, looking at how they acted to embed a 'societal view' among first-year graduates at UCD School of Business at University College, Dublin. They explain how this was achieved through the development of a module, assessed by case study evaluation and debate, which seeks to make students challenge their own assumptions about the role of business in society.

In Chapter 15, Baden discusses the integration of ethics into teaching at the School of Management at the University of South-ampton and discusses her approach of focusing on positive exam-ples of business behaviour, rather than citing examples of bad practice and corporate scandals, in order to encourage students to engage with the subject area. In something of a contrast, Christian, in Chapter 16, focuses on unsustainability, and bases his module on a field trip around Manchester for his students at Manchester Metropolitan University Business School, looking at the rivers and canals in the city to trace the history of Manchester and the Indus-trial Revolution, before examining examples of biodiversity and leading debates on the implications for society in the future. Chap-ter 17 features the work of Haloub and Beddewela from the Univer-sity of Huddersfield Business School, who describe how they set about creating ethical awareness in students through interactive group work, and focused on improving the critical thinking skills of their students. Stewart *et al.*, in Chapter 18, offer insight into the development of the MA in Leadership run by the School of Leadership, Organisations and Behaviour at Henley Business School, University of Reading. With the requirement of meeting the accreditation criteria set by the external bodies—AACSB, AMBA, EQUIS and PRME—using innovative teaching technologies, they give an honest assessment of the main features, outlining the successes and lessons learnt.

In Chapter 19, Thomson and Smith outline how the Glasgow School for Business and Society at Glasgow Caledonian University reviewed its curriculum to reflect PRME values. Module leaders were tasked with redesigning modules to embed PRME values. They go on to give details of one module redesign which includes a 'live' case story with the assistance of a local company whose directors gave briefings and where, once again, new technologies were employed to provide students with new methods of collaboration. Chapter 20 switches the focus to Birmingham, where Blewitt outlines Aston Business School's approach in developing its MSc in Social Responsibility and Sustainability. Conceived to be offered both as a full- and part-time programme, it was also offered as an online option. The challenges are identified and discussed along with one particular test: to communicate sustainability in 59 seconds! Chapter 21 looks at Durham University Business School's MBA programme where the International Enterprise Project challenges students to use their skills in real-life situations. Hirst explains that the project grew from the Sri Lankan tsunami of 2004, and since then students have been tasked to initiate projects themselves and bring them to fruition for the benefit of communities in the developing world.

The penultimate chapter (22), from Sunley, outlines the approach she took in developing a module which went on to win a 'Best Delivered Module of the Year' award in the Winchester University's Student Led Teaching Awards 2013/14. Rather than relying on an intellectual framework of conceptual knowledge and understanding as the basis for responsible management education, first-year business students were encouraged to engage with their own living experience of learning as stakeholders in the social, economic and environmental life of a virtual island that used an 'open source blogging platform'. This was utilised to develop a central narrative that challenged students to raise questions about sustainable business, ethical decision-making and the type of society they are prepared to support. The volume concludes with a chapter from Tadeka and Secchi outlining the approach taken to developing critical thinking skills in students from cultures where adopting the 'critical' standpoint is not an intuitive option.

Where are we going?

With the establishment of the UK and Ireland regional Chapter, the election of a Steering Committee with office bearers tasked with specific functions, a Secretariat with a paid administrator, and a website to support all the planned activities, we have levied a small charge on signatory schools. In the context, perhaps, of being part of the accreditation process for many schools, it represents a tiny proportion of the cost, and we believe that in the coming years, membership will be an important part of this process. However, it is important that we are also able to show, especially to those schools who are considering becoming signatories, what value there is in becoming part of this growing community. We hope that this publication will serve to fulfil this purpose and demonstrate how membership can stimulate change within schools and motivate colleagues and students alike to adopt a more responsible approach to what we do, embedding ethics and sustainability into our curricula.

Part A

Examining the values and mission of the school

1 *Educating responsible managers today for the global challenges of tomorrow*

Laura Davidson, Helyn Gould and Catherine Court

Strathclyde Business School

Glasgow, Scotland

Introduction

Strathclyde Business School's mission is to be an international school of useful learning for business and society. We value our strong international reputation for academic excellence, operate internationally and deliver our teaching portfolio with a global perspective.

As a Faculty of the University of Strathclyde, a leading technological university founded on John Anderson's principles, with a historic and distinctive mission to be a 'Place of Useful Learning', we aim to work for 'the public, for the good of mankind and the improvement of science'. Our purpose is to engage with and have an influence on business, organisational and public life, questioning convention and solving problems of significance to contemporary society. We pursue that mission by building on our enterprising history and realising the potential of the relationship between theory and practice to solve international problems by delivering:

- High quality research of **influence** to management practitioners, policy-makers and fellow researchers that is published in the best academic and practitioner journals and has high impact

- Educational programmes that are prized by students, alumni and employers alike for their **enterprising** and high quality learning experience delivering **globally** transferable knowledge and skills to our graduates
- Practical insight developed from close **engagement** with policy-makers, professionals and **international** partner organisations through our portfolio of knowledge exchange activities

Strathclyde Business School (SBS) has a long-established institutional commitment to making the skills, knowledge and resources of Strathclyde's academic and support staff available for the common good both academically and in the form of wider community contributions. SBS recognises the significance of responsible management and the increasing attention it is gaining in organisations across all sectors.

The School joined the Principles for Responsible Management Education in order to demonstrate to others the importance of being part of a body that promotes corporate responsibility and sustainability.

Challenge

Organisations seek flexible graduates who can adapt to change; are effective in operating in multi-disciplinary teams; have an awareness of ethical issues in business decision-making; and have well-developed interpersonal skills. This is the result of the growing recognition within organisations of the importance and benefits of responsible management.

SBS shares the belief that graduates should have these skills which have not been traditionally embedded in academic subjects, and the School has found it a challenge to design effective learning experiences which ensure the development of these skills for all students across its full undergraduate portfolio. With ten undergraduate principal subject pathways available, ranging from

Economics to Hospitality and Tourism Management, and with an intake of 450–500 students each year, the School recognised the need to revise the method by which it designs teaching and learning to account for the delivery of these skills. As a result, the School invested in a central programme, the Management Development Programme (MDP) to provide an intellectual and experiential spine to years 1–3 of the undergraduate degrees.

What we did

The MDP was introduced following a full revision of its predecessor programme which was introduced in 1999 to years 1–3 with an emphasis on the key skills agenda advocated by the report of the UK National Committee of Enquiry into Higher Education.

In 2011, the School established a working group with the remit to transform the programme from one initially designed to provide students with academic and ICT skills, to one which aims to enhance students' effectiveness and impact through experiential activities. The review saw a radical redesign of the programme's content, structure and delivery modes. The new MDP was designed to instil confidence and knowledge in students, develop critical skills, promote awareness of globalisation and ethical issues in personal and business decision-making, and provide the primary means for assurance of achieving those learning outcomes.

The revised programme saw business ethics and corporate social responsibility become its key learning outcomes, particularly in the first year when the theme was Social, Ethical and Environmental Governance (SEEG). The first semester examines the issues of SEEG, presented from different perspectives. The second semester is organised functionally, around what organisations do. Conceptual learning objectives for MDP1 include: globalisation, internationalisation and localisation; corporate social responsibility; organisational ethics and the third sector. Applied learning objectives include: emotional and social intelligence; team working skills; taking responsibility; and verbal and non-verbal communications skills. This understanding is gained through engagement with theory in parallel with examination of business case studies. Building on this, students are afforded the opportunity to enhance their understanding and knowledge of social responsibility and ethical issues in the subsequent 2 years of the programme. A developmental progress path in relation to these areas is demonstrated through the examination of real-life scenarios in the second year and then application of knowledge within the experiential learning environment in the third year whereby students gain direct experience of CSR and ethical issues in the working environment. Students can individualise their experience in the third year to suit their particular career ambitions by choosing from a number of options: international study experience; company internships; community engagement; business clinic; and research projects.

What happened

By widening its focus beyond the practical (i.e. beyond the teaching of basic academic skills), the School has been successful in giving the programme a much-needed transfusion of intellectual and entrepreneurial ideas. The remodelled MDP now develops students, both professionally and individually, so that they are better equipped to enter the workplace and make an immediate positive impact as responsible managers.

The School and students benefit from the involvement of major employers and alumni from all sectors with the MDP, participating in group sessions, observing business presentations and providing constructive feedback for students. The best teams are selected to present to senior staff in the sponsoring organisations (Deloitte, Procter & Gamble and Ernst & Young) and there are prizes for the best projects. Participating corporate contacts value the skills this programme brings to undergraduate students. Consequently, a number of students secure internships and full-time employment, as a result of their performance during MDP.

The first year of the MDP utilises a number of innovative delivery and assessment methods throughout the class, which have been identified as best practice within the university. The theoretical framework for each session is provided online through two short video lectures from one of the School's professors. Students are required to undertake a short task between lecture sessions and completion of these releases the second part of the video. In addition to this, prior to coming to the group session, students undertake some form of research in relation to a task set within the second video. This then forms the basis of activities during the group session and assessments, which include debates, presentations, research analysis, group discussion and report writing. As a result of the advanced preparation required by students, teaching sessions have become more engaged, with students having developed their conceptual thinking on relevant topics in advance of the class. The integration and development of skills relating to the business, personal and academic worlds are evident throughout the design.

The School is fully committed to supporting a student-led experience via the MDP; however, this results in a significant level of coordination and oversight at both the class and the pathway level to ensure a high standard of student experience and to maximise the educational benefit to our students. This requires central leadership by the MDP Director in collaboration with the academic departments and pathway leads; succession planning for these key roles is central to the ongoing success of the programme.

Delivery of the MDP can only be achieved in collaboration with external organisations, with employer input at all levels of the class (including in-class delivery). This presents challenges in terms of the management of relationships and coordination and timetabling of activities, and creates additional risk in the delivery of the programme. In conclusion, the School considers the introduction of the new MDP a success; feedback from students has been positive: they value the opportunity to gain confidence working in teams and presenting complex ideas to varied audiences. The feedback from industry partners such as Deloitte and Ernst & Young has recognised the outstanding quality of the work provided by our graduates, who are thinking about sustainable issues within the business context.

What next?

As with any new development, the School will continue to evaluate the success of the MDP against its objectives, to ensure the continuing refinement of the programme. This will allow us to continue to incorporate current thinking and developments in the areas of sustainability and responsible management.

In the short term, the School has developed and delivered a MOOC (massive open online course) through the Future Learn consortium. This MOOC, 'Understanding Modern Business and Organisations' has been developed based on materials taken from MDP1 and allows introductory access to SEEG issues outside of the traditional university community.

Discussions are under way across the university to provide access to the MDP beyond the Business School, to reach the scientists, engineers and policy-makers of the future.

2 *Gender equality in responsible management education and research*

Kathryn Haynes

Newcastle University Business School

Newcastle upon Tyne, England

Introduction

Newcastle University Business School's (NUBS) mission is to add value to all stakeholders by building excellence in teaching, research and engagement activity and to provide new, global perspectives and the inspiration to contribute to the responsible and ethical shaping of society. One such area where the School aims to make a contribution through its research, teaching and engagement activities, relates to **gender equality**.

Within the context of the university as a whole, Newcastle University is committed to the development of a fully inclusive university community which recruits and retains staff and students from all sectors of society. It aims to enable a positive and supportive culture that encourages everyone to flourish and reach their potential. It seeks to build strong positive relationships between staff, students and external stakeholders to promote a common vision where diversity is valued by all. It expects everyone to be treated with dignity and respect. This would also include the issue of gender equality.

Challenge

Gender *in*equality is pervasive throughout all societies and is recognised as a major impediment to poverty alleviation and sustainable development. The business sector, ranging from the smallest firms to the largest multinational corporations, can be responsible for causing, perpetuating and/or reducing gender inequality. The actions (or inactions) of business schools will play an important role in the education of future business leaders, policy-makers and decision-makers (Kilgour and Flynn 2012). Business schools can provide a leading role in challenging gender inequalities in a number of ways: through research which addresses the barriers, effects and outcomes of gender (in)equality; by educating students to understand, challenge and overcome stereotypical gendered assumptions; by providing role models and examples of good practices; and by engaging in debates on gender equality that can be transformative in the business world and society more generally.

Yet, business schools and academia more generally are not widely considered to be at the vanguard of gender equality. The most recent UK Higher Education Statistics Agency (HESA) *Staff in Higher Education Institutions* 2011/12 survey found that 55.5% of academic staff were men, and 44.5% women; 28.5% of male academic staff were employed part-time compared with 43.2% of women; and a higher proportion of women were also employed on fixed-term contracts. Moreover, despite a 4% rise in the number of female professors at UK universities last year, women hold fewer than 20% of senior academic posts. This is reflected in the position at Newcastle University Business School where under 15% of professors on permanent posts are women. In the business and management discipline generally, 89% of women academics earn less than £55,908 compared with 78% of men.[1]

1   HESA Staff in Higher Education Institutions survey 2011/12, Higher Education Statistics Agency, Cheltenham, Table 15: Academic staff (excluding atypical) by cost centre, mode of employment, salary range and gender 2011/12. https://www.hesa.ac.uk/publications-and-products

When we turn to the experience of students, there is a good gender mix on both undergraduate and postgraduate degree programmes. In terms of the types of roles and careers followed by business and management students, Newcastle University consistently has one of the best records for graduate employment in the UK. Within the first six months of graduating, 95.2 per cent of our 2012 UK and EU graduates entered employment or further study; more than three-quarters (84.9%) of those entering employment achieved a graduate level position.[2] However, they will be entering businesses, management positions and professions where there is still much to achieve in terms of gender equality in addressing the imbalance of women in senior positions, on corporate boards and in positions of power in wider society (Centre for Women and Democracy 2013).

Challenging gender inequalities and promoting gender equality

Newcastle University Business School challenges gender inequalities and promotes gender equality in a number of ways—through research, learning and teaching, and engagement—with PRME a key driver behind much of this activity.

Research

The Gender, Professions and Society (GPS) research group[3] was set up in 2012, taking an inter-disciplinary perspective on these three interrelated areas, subjecting the conduct and composition

2   Sourced from Destination of Leavers from Higher Education (DLHE) survey 2012–13, Higher Education Statistics Agency, Cheltenham. https://www.hesa.ac.uk/publications-and-products

3   Newcastle University Business School, 'Gender, Professions and Society (GPS)', www.ncl.ac.uk/nubs/research/centres/aga/gps/, accessed 26 June 2014.

of professions to scrutiny in terms of gender equality and social responsibility. It draws members from across the School, enabling members to integrate perspectives from economics, human resource management, organisation theory, and accounting and finance. Recent studies include: professional embodiment in the accountancy profession and the links between gender, identity and the body; women's promotion experiences in professional services firms; gender equality and sustainable development; women in management; working lives and graduate careers. Researchers engage with local government, professions, third sector organisations, corporations and academia, to address contemporary gender challenges in these fields. For example, the first Gender, Professions & Society Forum was held on 28 June 2013 at Newcastle University Business School, attracting delegates from academia, business and practice, debating women on boards, women's leadership in academia, and masculinity in the professions. Moreover, the GPS group, in conjunction with colleagues in the Human Resource Management research group, hosted Newcastle City Council's Open Policy Cabinet Meeting, 'Supporting Women in Employment: Working City and Reducing Inequality', led by Councillor Jane Streather of Newcastle City Council. The meeting explored the factors that continue to disadvantage women in employment at all levels of the job market and what can be done to tackle such barriers.

Learning and teaching

Students are encouraged to consider gender issues during their courses. For example, in the level 3 undergraduate module Accounting, Development & Change, for final year accounting students, historical and contemporary issues relating to gender and diversity issues in the accounting profession are a core part of the curriculum. Drawing from expertise within the School and published research by our staff (e.g. Haynes 2008, 2012), students analyse research papers that address these issues, enabling key theoretical perspectives and research to be applied to the learning and teaching context. Students are also encouraged to reflect on their own experiences where appropriate, and to consider how far and through what means gender equality issues have been or may be overcome in the accounting context. Gender of course relates to men as well as women, and in this sense the module engages both male and female students by asking them to reflect on the kind of professional, working life and personal life they aspire to.

Engagement

Other activities demonstrate active dialogue and engagement with relevant issues for PRME, particularly in this area of gender. For example Professor Kathryn Haynes presented at the 5th Annual Women's Empowerment Principles Event, Inclusion: Strategy for Change, in 2013, hosted by the United Nations and Deloitte at Rockerfeller Plaza, New York. The Women's Empowerment Principles (WEPs), initiated by the UN Global Compact and UN Women are a set of principles for business offering guidance on gender equality in the workplace, marketplace and community.

Together with Professors Pat Flynn, Bentley University USA, and Maureen Kilgour, Université de St-Boniface Canada, Haynes is co-facilitator of the PRME Gender Equality Working Group, whose mission is to bring together academics and employers in order to provide support and resources for integrating gender issues and awareness into management education, business school curricula, and related research to facilitate respect and support for the WEPs and PRME. The PRME Gender Equality Working Group has created a central, easily accessible repository of resources and information, designed to support the integration of gender issues into management education and research: for example, syllabi, case studies, journal articles and ongoing research.[4] The repository was launched at the PRME 3rd Global Forum in Rio in June 2012.

---

4   PRME, 'PRME Working Group on Gender Equality', www.unprme.org/
    working-groups/display-working-group.php?wgid=2715, accessed
    26 June 2014.

Integrating gender equality into management education

Such was the interest in the PRME Gender Equality Working Group repository and the challenges of bringing about gender equality facing both business and management educators and organisations themselves, that Greenleaf Publishing, in conjunction with PRME, commissioned a series of books on *Gender Equality as a Challenge for Business and Management Education*. The first, *Integrating Gender Equality into Management Education*, addresses the need to integrate gender equality into management education and provides examples of initiatives illustrating how this may occur from various disciplinary and global perspectives. The book provides conceptual and research rationales as to why responsible management education must address the issue of gender equality. It also identifies materials and resources that will assist faculty in integrating gender issues and awareness into a variety of disciplines and fields. The book is designed to help faculty integrate the topic of gender equality into their own teaching and gain support for the legitimacy of gender equality as an important management education topic in their institutions.

What next?

Gender inequality has a long history in the workplace, and traditions are hard to change. Many businesses and organisations are increasingly aware of the business case for promoting gender equality, both within and outside their organisational boundaries. Some evidence suggests that diversity in the workplace and gender equality boosts innovation and performance, and legal frameworks exist in many countries which mandate specific action on gender inequality in the workplace. However, critical issues remain: some disciplines remain resolutely gendered, affecting both men and women; case materials on women leaders and managers are still rare; and faculty are often unaware of how to access the related materials that do exist.

In the short term, the PRME Gender Equality Working Group is attempting to address these problems. Its second book, *Overcoming Challenges to Gender Equality in the Workplace*,[5] will address the challenges of achieving gender equality in the business and organisational context, and will be a collection of case studies, innovations and good practices, which illustrate initiatives and developments in gender equality in the workplace. In the longer term at Newcastle University Business School, gender equality will remain embedded as a key area of research, learning and teaching, and engagement.

References

Centre for Women and Democracy (2013) *Sex and Power 2013: Who Runs Britain?* (London: Counting Women In coalition, Centre for Women and Democracy, the Electoral Reform Society, the Fawcett Society, the Hansard Society and Unlock Democracy).

Haynes, K. (2008) '(Re)figuring Accounting and Maternal Bodies: The Gendered Embodiment of Accounting Professionals', *Accounting, Organizations and Society* 33.4/5: 328-48.

Haynes, K. (2012) 'Body Beautiful?: Gender, Identity and the Body in Professional Services Firms', *Gender, Work & Organization* 19.5: 489-507.

Kilgour, M., and P. Flynn (2012) *PRME Working Group on Gender Equality Working Paper* (New York: PRME). Available at http://prmegenderequalityworkinggroup.unprme.wikispaces.net/Welcome+to+the+Wikispace

5   PRME, call for contributions, www.unprme.org/resource-docs/PRME Book2Callforcontributionsfinal.pdf, accessed 26 June 2014.

3 *Building excellence as an internationally recognised business school*

Jane Gibbon and Kathryn Haynes

Newcastle University Business School

Newcastle upon Tyne, England

Introduction

Newcastle University Business School (NUBS) first signed a commitment to the Principles for Responsible Management Education (PRME) in December 2009 and has consolidated and affirmed its responsibility in two Sharing Information on Progress (SIP) reports.

In today's global business environment, a good management education can provide a crucial foundation on which to build a better world. NUBS continues to develop its provision to support new generations of leaders who will address the increasingly complex challenges that are faced by society. NUBS is committed to providing management education that responds to these ever-increasing demands. The banking crisis of 2007–08 and recent corporate governance scandals provide examples of how conventional approaches to business education can no longer meet the needs of the marketplace.

The School has recently revised its vision, mission and values, strengthening its commitment to responsible management education. The vision and mission incorporate the need to be innovative and are reinforced through four values that characterise all NUBS' activities. These four values are: conscientiousness and integrity; curiosity and openness; critical relevance; and creativity in all areas.

The particular achievements that demonstrate a commitment to PRME during the last two years are: the continued development of engagement with all stakeholders; the School's contribution to the university's societal themes of Sustainability and Social Renewal; activities within academic subject groups; developments within the teaching provision; and current research and publications from research groups.

NUBS has developed a strong vision that embraces the core of PRME through the aspiration to be an internationally recognised business school. Its aim is to have a world-leading research reputation across a range of disciplines, including: critical accounting; economics; human resources management; innovation systems; services marketing; and strategy, organisations and society. The School will further develop its distinctive pedagogy based on the 'Theory of Application' approach, incorporating a more blended learning style and a commitment to lifelong learning, producing a student experience that is highly rewarding and challenging. It continues to work with partners and external organisations, from international corporates to local voluntary organisations, to both develop and strengthen the commitment to PRME.

Challenge

Newcastle University prides itself as being a world-class civic university, by which we mean responding to the needs and demands of civil society and serving as a public good. As a civic university with a global reputation for academic excellence, Newcastle University is committed to solving, rather than describing, the great challenges of our age, and thus helping to frame a more optimistic global debate.

Newcastle University's motto is 'Excellence with a purpose'. The commitment of Newcastle University Business School in being a signatory to the Principles for Responsible Management Education (PRME) demonstrates this purpose. Newcastle University is a civic university with a role to play in society by bringing both research and teaching to bear on issues faced by local, national or international communities.

In response to the great challenges of our age Newcastle University has three Societal Challenge Themes and is committed to ensuring that the outcomes of research help to address some of the key global issues by focusing on these themes as part of our overall focus on excellence with impact. The research, teaching and engagement activities of Newcastle University Business School are closely linked to the three Societal Challenge Themes of Ageing, Social Renewal and Sustainability. These three themes address the demand side of research by responding to some of the most pressing needs within society.

What we did

Newcastle University Business School has taken the role of the civic university as a key focus by incorporating the values of global social responsibility, as portrayed in international initiatives such as the United Nations Global Compact, into academic activities and curricula. One development within the School was to revise the vision, mission and values of the School in order to reflect and underpin the School's commitment to being a signatory of PRME. The process of consultation resulted in the following vision, mission and values for the School[1]:

Vision

To be an internationally recognised business school by being regionally rooted, nationally influential and globally respected.

Mission

We add value to all stakeholders through building excellence in teaching, research and engagement activity and provide new, global perspectives and the inspiration to contribute to the responsible and ethical shaping of society.

1   http://www.ncl.ac.uk/nubs/about/missionandvision.htm

Values:
Conscientiousness and integrity

In everything we do, we strive to change the world for the better, through socially and ethically responsible practice and respect for fellow human beings. We are aware of the impact our work has on the world around us and are deliberate in the relationships we forge and sustain on behalf of our staff, students, and stakeholders.

Curiosity and openness

We encourage open minds and a fascination around the edges, as well as the traditional core, of business education. In an ever-changing world, our students and staff must be ready to embrace innovation, take action, and work across disciplines to see beyond the accepted norms.

Critical relevance

Through our research, teaching and engagement, we reflect upon those critical perspectives that influence global policy and practice. We demonstrate relevance and value in an external context by thinking critically and engaging with new ideas.

Creativity in all areas

We value creative, collaborative approaches to work inside and outside the traditional university environments. Taking inspiration from the worlds of practice, especially the technological and design-led arenas, we will seek innovative ways of teaching, learning, and applying our theory into practice.

What happened

The challenge was how to incorporate the vision, mission and values across a large and diverse School so that it is embedded in our learning, teaching and student experience and in our research and partnerships.

Learning, teaching and student experience

Newcastle University Business School is organised around four subject areas: Accounting and Finance; Economics; Leadership, Work and Organisation; and Marketing, Operations and Systems. Through the subject areas, NUBS provides a diverse and complex provision of programmes that provide strong links to the issues and demands of managing organisations and the social and environmental impacts of all business enterprises. An example of added value and good practice in relation to student experience is the Global Experience Opportunities offered to NUBS' students, enabling them to take part in unique opportunities to ensure they have a broader globally responsible perspective in an ever-changing world. The opportunities support them in achieving their career aspirations and internationalise their student experience. The Global Experience Opportunity is an easily accessible offering to all students across the School and introduces them to the international business community while developing practical skills needed to succeed in global markets. Other opportunities open to students are summer internships, summer school programmes, 12 month placements, global competitions and global study opportunities.

Research

NUBS is part of a research-intensive university and there is a thriving research community with links extending across the world. Research is of key importance to all activities within the School where:

- It is a vital part of the contribution made by members of the School to develop better understanding of the issues facing managers, professionals and policy-makers
- It is central to how the School can engage directly with organisations and policy-makers at regional, national and international levels

- It provides the foundation for teaching at all levels, ensuring that students are exposed to knowledge and approaches that reflect the latest thinking and are grounded in practice

Since the Business School was formed, the focus has been on conducting and disseminating research of the highest international standard, which contributes to and influences policy and practice.

The School's research activity is conducted through Research Groups; the work that supports PRME is primarily conducted within the following research groups[2]:

- Centre for Knowledge, Innovation, Technology and Enterprise (KITE)
- Accounting, Governance and Accountability (AGA)
- Economics
- Gender, Professions and Society
- Human Resource Management, Work and Employment (HRMWE)
- Services Marketing
- Strategy, Organizations and Society (SOS)

Partnerships

Partners are another key element of the School's work; the International Advisory Board (IAB) has supported Newcastle over a number of years. Its role is to help bring the School's vision to life, provide strategic guidance and, importantly, independent advice and sound judgement. Members of the IAB represent strands of the renewed vision, and are all highly accomplished and experienced people in their own fields. The rich mixture of diverse talent is of tremendous value to the School as their knowledge and skills, grounded in the realities of business management, academic and public life, provide a great sounding board for the Business School. Members' networks further enhance the excellent links, active dialogue and engagement the School already has with the business community.

2   http://www.ncl.ac.uk/nubs/research/centres/

NUBS is also sponsoring the North East Institute of Business Ethics (NIBE), which was created in 2013, linking NUBS' Ethics Forum with a widely representative group of regional business people. This partnership supports NIBE as an independent regional resource overseen by an influential cross-sector steering group with an aspiration to become a focal point for good business behaviour.

The David Goldman Visiting Professorship in Innovation and Enterprise is another key partnership for the School. The position is awarded each year to a leading entrepreneur or business leader from within the region who provides inspiration and motivation to budding entrepreneurs and business leaders. The role involves working with the School to provide leadership and mentoring to students and faculty, and also delivering the David Goldman Annual Business School Lecture.

What next?

NUBS plans to continue and extend the commitment to PRME by further embedding the work already being conducted across research, teaching and learning, and engagement activities. These activities are closely linked to all the work involved with the accreditation bodies: AACSB (Association of Advance Collegiate Schools of Business); AMBA (Association of MBAs); and EFMD (European Foundation for Management Development Programme Accreditation System).

As a signatory to the UK and Ireland Chapter of PRME, NUBS supports the development of PRME within UK business schools. The support is expected to be through attendance at Chapter meetings, hosting seminars, workshops and invited speaker events, as well as continually working on embedding the PRME principles into all activities.

The Global Experience initiative will provide a key contribution in extending the programme of internationalisation for teaching and learning. The plan is to further enhance and extend these initiatives in the future.

NUBS will continue to bring together business leaders, students and academics through initiatives to develop further links for dialogue, research and engagement. NUBS is committed to educating responsible business leaders and global citizens who are equipped to manage in future business environments that are global, complex and sustainable. The School is committed to developing the potential of its students by providing them with a sound theoretical and practical training that focuses on innovative thinking, entrepreneurship, accountability, governance, ethics and social responsibility. The School believes that this can be achieved through teaching, research and engagement within a business school that strives to implement sustainable and ethical practices.

Part B

Developing centres
and outreach initiatives
embedding the values
of PRME

4 *The New Romantics of responsible leadership*

Steve Kempster and Emma Watton

Lancaster University Management School

Lancaster, England

Introduction

The Lancaster Leadership Centre (LLC) has been established within the Lancaster University Management School (LUMS) for 10 years. It has acted as a hub of enquiry, research, teaching and leadership development activity within LUMS. In 2014 the LLC will host the *6th Developing Leadership Capacity Conference*. This case story describes the process for creating a conference themed on responsible leadership which is intended to enable a series of outcomes: a rich and diverse engagement from conference presenters; acting as a catalyst for the relaunch of the LLC towards responsible leadership with its aligned MSc programme; creating interest internally and externally on the theme of responsible leadership; and facilitate broader university engagement on initiatives such as Principles for Responsible Management Education (PRME) and the Global Responsible Leadership Initiative (GRLI).

Challenge

There was a strong belief that when the LLC was relaunched it would have at its heart a raison d'être centred on responsible leadership with a focus that supports the suggestion by Kofi Annan of 'a move from value to values, from shareholders to stakeholders, and from balance sheets to balanced development'[1] (14 October 2002).

It was felt that this narrative would enable a resonant interaction with students, researchers, visiting academics, the business community and the wider societies that the LLC serves. In addition the LLC would be able to connect to an existing global partnership network of HEIs (higher education institutions) and affiliations such as the International Leadership Association. Thus an international reach could be established enabling a rapid and broad engagement through responsible leadership.

Although the School is most active in this important area at both a local and a global level, a period of internal dialogue and collaboration enabled the development of a range of ideas to support the LLC. The ideas included offering to host the *Developing Leadership Capacity Conference*, the development of a new MSc pathway and to make recommendations on joining relevant international initiatives—PRME is one of the options being considered. For the purposes of this case story we will focus on the conference as an example of organising a research event aligned to the PRME principles.

What we did

With support from the dean a budget was secured internally to ease the costs of running the *Developing Leadership Capacity*

---

[1]   GRLI call for engagement document 2005:6 available at http://www.grli .org/index.php/component/docman/cat_view/13-source-documents

Conference, particularly the costs needed to invite an international line-up of keynote speakers. A working party of 'enthusiasts' was brought together to create a theme for the conference: 'The New Romantics of Responsible Leadership'. This afforded us the opportunity to explore contemporary debates in the leadership field that are placing a greater emphasis on leadership as process and outcome, leadership as practice, leadership as a relational and collaborative dynamic, and leadership as authentic, ethical and societally purposeful.

The New Romantics theme was augmented by the LLC's close proximity to the English Lake District and the works of the poet William Wordsworth. Wordsworth and other notable poets of the late 18th and early 19th century such as Byron, Coleridge and Shelley became recognised for a pioneering and romantic style of writing that celebrated nature and the spirit of the individual; an emphasis on place and creativity, on vocation and purpose. Their poems and ideals were a sharp contrast to the harshness of the industrial world around them.

The similarity between the current global challenges we face coupled with a renewed calling for leadership to have ideals of purpose, ethics, creativity, idealism and calling at its heart were seen as highly desirable for the conference. A pre-conference reflective walk aims to explore leadership 'spots of time' with conference participants. The walk creates an interdisciplinary connection through an academic colleague in the English Department who relates Wordsworth's poems and life experiences with contemporary leadership thinking—most notably on calling and purpose.

What happened

The conference call for papers generated much interest from academics and researchers from around the world. Several people provided feedback on the relevance and appeal of the call which had deep resonance with them.

The conference call generated submissions from 25 different HEIs drawn from seven countries. Mapping the HEIs represented to those already signed up as signatories to PRME shows that 36% of the submissions are from PRME-active institutions. This perhaps helps to demonstrate the close alignment of the PRME principles to the focus of the conference. In a sense both affirming the importance of such a themed conference in creating ongoing research and networking opportunities, and also speaking to a greater narrative purpose in aligning research interests that may otherwise have remained isolated and fragmented.

We hope to continue momentum from the conference by selecting some of the papers being presented to be included in an edited volume on 'The New Romantics of Leadership' to be published by Routledge in 2014.

What next?

Through the success of the conference we hope to generate further interest in the topic of responsible leadership. We envisage this interest to be multi-faceted. Internally, we anticipate that it will aid us in the application for membership of both PRME and the GRLI in the short term. We also hope it will generate new PhD and research opportunities across LUMS and more broadly with conference participants. Externally, we see it as the first step in the relaunch of the LLC and a set of activities, including the new MSc in Leadership Practice and Responsibility, that we are hopeful will create responsible leadership of the future.

This case story illustrates the importance of aligning research with education. In particular it highlights the importance of enabling colleagues to connect ideas and debates with regard to responsible leadership with activities and initiatives for developing responsible management education in their respective business schools.

5 Curriculum development: engaging students in local charity/community projects

Sachiko Takeda and Carly Lamont

The Business School, Bournemouth University

Bournemouth, England

Introduction

Bournemouth University, located in south of England, is committed to the region but with an outlook that is truly global. The Business School became a signatory to the Principles for Responsible Management Education (PRME) in 2009. Joining the initiative was part of the School's endeavour to pursue responsible management education, which has been rapidly increasing in significance for educating the next generation of business leaders. Every year, the School welcomes approximately 250 undergraduate Business Studies students. Guided by the PRME Principles—to develop the capabilities of students while keeping the values of social responsibility at the centre of academic activities and curriculum—all Business Studies students take a management ethics module following enrolment. The responsible management education continues with approximately half of these students opting in to study environmental/global sustainability in their second year. A module dealing with corporate social responsibility is then taken by all management students in their final year before they move into the business world.

Challenge

The modules mentioned above start by engaging students with conceptual and theoretical discourse surrounding business ethics, sustainability and social responsibility, and subsequently require them to apply the theories to real cases with critical analyses. However, the modules do not provide students with opportunities to learn through action and experience. Although most of the students gain such experience through a work placement in their third year, engagement with experiences that are strongly related to social responsibility at a much earlier stage of study would be desirable for more effective learning. This would provide the students, from the first weeks of their university studies, with a solid foundation on which to build responsible management knowledge and understanding throughout their undergraduate programme. In order to fully address the 'Purpose' aspect of the PRME Principles and fully develop the capabilities of students to be future generators of sustainable value for business and society at large, it is necessary to create educational frameworks that provide effective learning experiences for responsible leadership, as set out in the PRME Principles. At the same time, while globalisation and multinational corporations' business conduct are often emphasised in the School's framework of responsible management education, commitment to the sustainability-related activities of the local community needs to be addressed to a greater extent; this is related to the PRME Principles of "Partnership" and "Dialogue".

What we did

Addressing the challenge outlined above, a module was introduced which required all first-year Business Studies students to engage in managing community projects in the first term. The coursework includes the following:

- *Preparatory reference to policies and regulations (individual task).* Students are required to know and understand the university's institutional policies and regulations and complete an online test to demonstrate their ability to comply. This is to enhance understanding of students who have just entered the university and make them aware they are interacting with local organisations as ambassadors of the Business School and the University.
- *Managing local community projects (group task).* Students are asked to organise two events to support the local community. Although the tutors and other supporting staff from the Student Union provide guidance and advice, students are expected to carry out their own research on the conventions and best practices in developing the events:

    Event 1. Students as a group organise a fundraising event for a charity. The type of event and charity to support is decided through consensus within the seminar groups. All funds raised are donated to the relevant local charity through the Student Union.

    Event 2. Students as a group support and contribute to one community-based project. Students choose a project they would like to carry out from a list of options provided by the Student Union Volunteering.

    Students are requested to record the details of the events on the online discussion forum prepared for the module. The documentation should include:

    1. *Goal and objectives.* Each team should come up with their own goal statement supported by a set of objectives for the project.

    2. *Organisational chart.* The roles (e.g. project manager, communication officer, etc.) and responsibilities within the team are presented in a form of organisational chart.

3. *Stakeholder analysis.* Students are asked to identify all the stakeholders of each event and analyse their interests/needs, associated risks and the way they could be affected by the event.

4. *Project plan.* All steps within the project have to be graphically presented with a chart, indicating dependencies between the tasks, deadlines and resources.

5. *Risk assessment.* A risk assessment needs to be completed for each event, taking into considerations all stakeholders.

6. *Project log.* Students are required to keep the full documentation of the management of each event, including correspondences with the local charities, meeting agendas and minutes.

7. *Final event report and team evaluation.* The final report includes the evaluation of the teamwork and team members' level of contribution, each event's video documentary or narrated presentation slideshow, and a mock-up newspaper article.

- *A reflective account (individual task).* Each student reflects on what they learned through the experience of engaging in fundraising for a local charity and managing a community-based project.

This core module runs concurrently with a module of management ethics. All Business Studies students in Bournemouth University are therefore taught responsible management, both theoretically and empirically, immediately upon entering the university.

What happened

Every year, students organise a variety of fundraising events to support charity organisations: for example, a cake sale and competition in support of breast cancer; an event to raise awareness of men's health in support of prostate cancer; a car wash event in support of Children in Need; or a food collection event in support of a local homeless shelter organisation—to name a few. One year, a group raised £1,350 by completing a cycle ride from Bournemouth to Paris on exercise bikes. In 2013 the business students raised a total of £3,622 through their fundraising projects. Many students said they found the tasks interesting and stimulating, and learned the importance of being proactive.

However, the students found some aspects of the projects particularly challenging. Firstly, teamworking presented a few problems to some students. Students commented that, whereas teamwork provided a sense of belonging/ownership and motivation towards the team effort, apathy from some members was difficult to manage, resulting in conflicts. Secondly, while students identified communication to be the key to success, communication between the local charity organisations and students was at times problematic. For instance, students did not find out that the expectations of the charities exceeded their abilities, impacting on the feasibility of the project in the given timeframe. In other cases, communication was too slow or too late which put some stakeholders under pressure. Coordinating public fundraising events with the local Council also posed challenges concerning health and safety issues.

Nevertheless, students' reflective accounts revealed that overall they had a positive learning experience throughout the module. Many students identified the benefits of the business community engagement activities and the impact such activities had on their transition into university life. Teamwork also helped them to bond with each other and increase their level of self-confidence. Positive comments included: 'the module significantly helped us prepare for our future professional lives' and 'giving something back to the local community was very satisfying'. Many found the projects extremely rewarding and some subsequently joined volunteer teams at the university. One student commented: 'the experience changed my mind-set for life!'

What next?

In order to encourage more initiative from students, we intend to no longer offer them a selection of community-based projects to choose from. In future they will make first contact with local charity organisations and coordinate projects with them. This is expected to enhance our efforts towards the partnership and dialogue aspects of the PRME Principles while, at the same time, further develop students' sustainability and social responsibility values through effective learning experiences. We are also planning to prepare an experience-based module for second-year students in order to ensure the continuity of effective learning.

6 *Fostering PRME partnerships and constant dialogue*

Karen Blakeley

Winchester Business School
Winchester, England

Introduction

For many schools the first stage in the adoption of the Principles is an examination of the curriculum, and this is reflected in the narratives of many of the Sharing Information on Progress (SIP) reports that have already been submitted. As a relatively newly established business school, we were able to design our curriculum with the Principles in mind which we now review on a regular basis to ensure that the content reflects the values of our university and the Principles, which are so closely aligned.

Initially we examined each of the Principles in turn and took steps to engage with the rationale behind them. In looking at Principle 5 we perceived a number of challenges, and set about creating an approach which would produce all-round benefits from fostering partnerships with business and the wider community.

The Hoare Centre for Responsible Management

First, we had to decide what we were seeking to achieve, and decided that the aim of the initiative would be threefold, and ambitious:

1. To build an emergent community of informed minds
2. To create a forum where issues of significant societal importance could be debated
3. To establish an entity with the potential to inform thoughts and activities, reflecting the aims of the PRME initiative, over the long term

In essence, the aim was to create and sustain a 'Community of Practice' founded on the values of PRME involving faculty from the Business School and the wider university, businesses of all sizes, civil society organisations and our students.

Second, we perceived that to make a success of such an initiative, its launch and subsequent development would be greatly aided by the support of a high-profile sponsor.

Challenge

We considered the obstacles to developing a vibrant, dynamic and effective community of practice and identified three key challenges to our plans:

- How to identify the most suitable partner?
- How to persuade the partner to provide financial support?
- How to develop a series of events to fulfil the aims?

What we did

First of all we worked up our proposal by carefully constructing a business plan to ensure our funding arrangements were adequate, and that we could demonstrate both to the university and to the prospective partner that the proposal was viable and fully thought through. The plan was presented to the dean of the school who obtained support from the university to approach suitable partners. We then identified a charitable trust with connections to Winchester and the university and an approach was made, with a positive response from the trust.

By this time a 'wish-list' had been drawn up of events with high-profile speakers actively engaged in promoting CSR and a plan to attract local businesses and NGOs was presented to the trustees. An annual series of events, talks and workshops was developed and two programmes planned at a provisional level. Initially it was envisaged that there would be a more regional focus, but that as the Centre's reputation increased and its activities became better understood, national figures would be contacted and asked to participate. The trust agreed to back the proposal with funding sufficient to back the activities of the Centre for five years.

The Centre was launched in 2011 and the programme of events was circulated to a database of regional companies and organisations within a 25 mile radius. Since then its activities have increased and two years later, a Chair in Responsible Management was supported by the trust, and an appointment made in December 2012.

What happened

Relationships

This initiative has allowed the Business School to develop useful relationships with businesses at a local and national level. Equally, however, multinational businesses with facilities in the vicinity (e.g. IBM, Kingfisher Group) have been supportive and provided speakers for several events. A thriving network is developing with new ideas for further events originating from this interaction.

Networks

As these relationships developed so other networks engaged with the activities of the Centre, and the Centre continued to broaden its reach. The university embraced the initiative and joined Business in the Community as a full member. In fact, the deputy vice-chancellor was invited to sit on the Regional Advisory Board of BiTC, a position since taken up by the newly appointed Chair in Responsible Management.

The university also became a full member of the UK Network of the Global Compact, and work is now under way to involve all faculties in the university with the goals and ideals of the Global Compact.

The Business School profile

As a Business School which was only established in 2008, it was seen as a crucial part of the process of increasing its visibility, reputation and reach that the Centre's CSR activities should become widely known, and its activities have an appeal to a wide range of interested stakeholders. With the appointment of a professor attached to the Centre, the task now is to build on the successes of the initial two years, and to begin to develop a centre of excellence. Already initiatives are under way to increase the number of visiting fellows and professors attached to the Centre to foster increasing interest in the Centre's activities both locally and nationally.

Enhancing the student experience

The relationships which have been nurtured and the networks that have been developed have acted to enrich the experience of students at the School by allowing us access to a growing pool of CSR expertise in both small and large businesses as well as social enterprises and NGOs, who willingly visit classes and take part in teaching activities as well as providing materials for case studies. This activity has also increased the range and number of different possibilities for student placements and research dissertation opportunities.

The significance of PRME

- PRME provides a readily identifiable, proven framework through which to reach out to interested companies and organisations to develop a mutual understanding of the challenges and possible approaches to achieving sustainability
- PRME stand behind the activities of Winchester Business School and are easy reference points as we plan activities going forward
- Stakeholders understand more quickly how the university values are being operationalised though the Principles and the Global Compact

7 PRME and the Centre for Sustainable and Resilient Communities

John Lever, Adrian Wood, Julia Meaton and Walter Mswaka

University of Huddersfield Business School

Huddersfield, England

Introduction

The University of Huddersfield Business School recently established a new Centre for Sustainable and Resilient Communities. This builds on a long tradition of engagement in this area, dating back to 1994 when Professor Richard Welford directed the Centre for Corporate Environmental Management and the subsequent emergence of the Centre for Enterprise, Ethics and the Environment. These earlier Centres worked on corporate environmental issues but broadened their remit to address wider issues of environmental management and planning within local, regional and global communities.

The new Centre thus builds on a long tradition of research concerning the links between businesses, organisations, ethics and the environment. It brings together and develops synergies among a range of research projects in the areas of sustainability and resilience. This research underpins a range of teaching in the School and ensures that many of the principles of PRME are/will be taught explicitly and implicitly across a number of courses focused on the concept of an **inclusive and sustainable global economy** (Principle 1).

Challenge

The Business School has been engaging with sustainability and ethical issues for nearly 20 years since the BA (Hons) in Business Studies with Environmental Management was first introduced. More recently, the School has embraced the need for all Business Studies students to understand the concepts and implications of sustainability. All students are now taught a six-week programme covering sustainability, ethical and responsible management and issues of global equity.

All undergraduate programmes in the School have optional ethical and environmental management options, and these are compulsory for those on the Business Studies with Environmental Management programme. All lecturers have been tasked with introducing elements of sustainability and responsibility into their modules so that these themes are woven into the student learning experience. We are moving forward by more fully integrating responsible management into the teaching programme and courses are being redesigned to more fully reflect the PRME agenda.

At undergraduate level we have specific courses on:

- Corporate Social Responsibility
- Environmental Management
- Contemporary Issues in Business
- Environmental Policy
- Business Responsibility and Sustainability

At postgraduate level this leads into the MSc Risk, Disaster and Environmental Management. This course looks at a wide range of risks in business, organisational and geographical environments and equips students with the ability to identify, assess and manage these risks. The disaster management element of the course develops students' ability to analyse the consequences when things go wrong, and gives them the practical skills for disaster prevention, preparedness, mitigation and management. The course is underpinned by the need to understand the environment and its interface with human activity in recognition of the fact that many of the greatest threats in the 21st century are related to the environment, and that many human-induced disasters go on to impact the natural environment, often with further negative feedback for humans.

The MSc balances academic theory with practical skills and provides students with a vocational set of skills that they can apply in their working environments. This innovative Master's degree reflects the belief that emergencies of any kind normally require inter-disciplinary understanding and inter-organisational cooperation, and that a multi-disciplined approach is essential in order to understand and meet the unusual demands of unwelcome and unexpected events. This means empowering agencies, organisations and businesses through the coordination of expertise from appropriate business, academic, governmental and humanitarian personnel and encouraging better coordination and understanding between all stakeholders in society in the event of an unexpected incident of whatever nature.

The MSc is strongly linked to the Centre for Sustainable and Resilient Communities and much of the ongoing research within the research centre is directly linked to the teaching on the programme. Modules on the MSc include:

- Principles of Environmental Management
- Sustainable Business
- Principles of Risk
- Corporate Governance and Ethics

At present, the Centre also supports some 14 doctoral students from six countries. Current areas under investigation by doctoral students include:

- Sustainable tourism
- Forest and land management
- Corporate social responsibility
- Social marketing
- Land use planning

- Education for sustainable development
- Honey value chain

What we did

Research in the Centre aims to produce case studies and material that can facilitate the teaching of PRME at undergraduate and post-graduate levels. Examples of our research and their relevance are:

- Climate change and the use of seasonal wetlands for rural business and livelihoods in Malawi
- Forest enterprise development to enhance the value of tropical rainforests in Ethiopia
- Research on refugees and sustainability in housing in Jordan to identify new methods of overcoming impasses in planning
- Addressing the challenge of promoting animal welfare globally as a key component of sustainability
- Developing new approaches to local resilience in the UK

What happened

Students on the MSc are having applicable learning experiences for responsible leadership (Principle 3). They are being taught how to undertake ISO14001 and ISO26000 and develop the skills to lead initiatives addressing corporate environmental and CSR agendas.

In line with the emergence of the Business Benchmark for Animal Welfare (BBFAW) undergraduate and postgraduate students are being introduced to the importance of animal welfare and bio-sustainabilities for business, environmental and human health. Drawing on recent research across a number of European countries, students are examining how the responsible management of animal welfare by large global retailers and food corporations can increase profits *and* improve sustainability outcomes across the three pillars of sustainable development.

Rural enterprise development through natural resources has considerable potential to raise the value of resources, such as forests, and make them valuable resources for communities, which in turn may lead to changes in behaviour towards more sustainable use. These ideas are behind field research projects in Ethiopia and Malawi, where work is undertaken with local NGOs. This feeds into various case study materials for use in teaching.

What next?

Over the coming years we plan to develop strategies to help raise self and global awareness in undergraduate and postgraduate students so that they become responsible managers through the dissemination of our research insights to managers across all sectors (Principles 5).

We are developing a range of ways to pursue debate and engage policy-makers through our research. This is already being done in the southern region of Ethiopia through forest policy to support sustainable forest enterprise development through Participatory Forest Management (Principle 6). Further development of our work in Ethiopia will explore the role of enterprise development in different facets of the landscape in part of Ethiopia, leading to an eco-region approach to economic development that ensures environmentally sustainable regional development.

Our research on refugees and sustainability in housing in Jordan is directly linked to management issues and seeks to identify new methods of overcoming impasses in planning for long-term displaced people. The lessons from this research could have significant relevance in the future when economic and environmental refugees are predicted to increase.

The Centre is currently developing work on the cultural aspects of disaster management. This will enable effective management practices to be developed that will address the needs of different cultures and ethnicities around the world, resulting in more effective and culturally relevant principles and practices.

In the UK, we are currently perusing opportunities with a number of local authorities to foster new management agendas to help nurture local resilience. Further work is planned to investigate animal welfare in line with the expansion of international halal markets and sustainability discourses.

Conclusion

The emergence of the PRME principles coincides with an important and significant phase of development in the Centre for Sustainable and Resilient Communities at the University of Huddersfield Business School. The principles are a useful guide to our research and teaching that will help us to develop the capacity of our students to be responsible stewards of a sustainable global economy.

8 *Young and unlimited, realising talent: Kemmy Business School's programmes with local schools*

Briga Hynes, Stephen Kinsella and Sheila Killian

Kemmy Business School, University of Limerick

Limerick, Republic of Ireland

Introduction

Kemmy Business School (KBS) at the University of Limerick has been a member of PRME since 2008, and recently joined both the PRME Champions group and the UK and Ireland regional PRME Chapter. The principles and spirit of PRME are integral to the ethos of the School. Our mission statement commits us to operating in a socially engaged environment, and one of the four strategic goals of the school is to provide leadership in economic, social and community development. This emphasis arises from the leg-acy of the late Jim Kemmy, after whom the School is named. Jim Kemmy spent his life working for the betterment of all in society and the School's mission statement is an ongoing reminder of the power of education as a contributor to social good as well to eco-nomic prosperity. He was also an inspirational figure, and we aim, through the programmes described here, to provide such inspira-tion for local teenagers, encouraging them not to feel limited in their personal ambition.

Challenge

Limerick has a high degree of social and economic disadvantage concentrated in several areas of the city in particular, compared with populations of similar size across Ireland (Hourigan, 2011). Youth unemployment in 2014 is estimated at 49%, while a recent analysis of social class structure (based on occupational group-ings) by area shows the largest proportions in so-called 'regenera-tion' areas belonged to the lower social classes (semi-skilled and unskilled occupations) while the largest proportion in other areas belonged to the higher social classes (professional/managerial and technical). The average level of education in regeneration levels is lower to upper secondary (Humphreys *et al.*, 2012).

Social welfare payments are the largest source of household income in the regeneration areas of the city (Humphreys *et al.*, 2012). Schools in regeneration areas are generally designated DEIS (Deliv-ering Equality of Opportunity in Schools), meaning they receive more in state support, especially with respect to early school leaver programmes, youth reach schemes, home school commu-nity liaison schemes, and school completion programmes. Smyth (1999), McCoy *et al.* (2010), O'Connell *et al.* (2006) and McCoy and Smyth (2011) have all found persistent evidence of social inequal-ity prevalent in higher education participation in Ireland.

Faced with a series of interlocking social and economic prob-lems, every report urges better integration of services across state agencies and educational institutions. Here we provide two exam-ples of such collaborations.

What we did

KBS undertook two targeted initiatives, described below, partner-ing with DEIS schools at both primary and secondary level.

CAA

The Centre for Academic Achievement (CAA) is a collaboration between the Centre for Talented Youth (Ireland) and KBS. The overarching idea was to bring KBS's faculty expertise and the University of Limerick's student experience to Limerick's DEIS school population using courses which could grab students' imaginations.

The CAA programme is a 6-week long, after-school academic enrichment programme of the type pioneered by Healion (2013). Each course focuses on increasing self-esteem for disadvantaged students aged 8–12, which it is hoped will lead to better outcomes in their mainstream classes. The programme places a strong emphasis on increasing the linkages between schools, school completion programmes and the University of Limerick.

Through the University's Access Office, students are nominated by their school to take part in the programme. Students self-select into a variety of courses, including forensic science, medicine, horrid histories, how to make an app, movie animation, chemistry, engineering and investigative science. In the 2013/2014 academic year 203 students will take part in the programme.

ICE

The Innovation, Creativity and Entrepreneurship (ICE) programme was developed in partnership with local DEIS school, Colaiste Chiaráin, and is delivered by their teachers to students aged 12 to 15. The novel curriculum enables the students to explore their own imaginations, entrepreneurial interests and talents, and equips them with the skills they need to be college- and career-ready. The focus is on personal development, opportunity recognition and personal reflection as well as business ideas and business plans, building the esteem and life skills of the students and expanding their ambition and self-reliance.

While the programme is delivered by the school, KBS took a lead in designing content, structure and assessments. Some KBS faculty are also involved in team teaching, and ongoing mentoring sessions and training workshops are arranged for teachers in the various ICE subject areas. The teaching methods emphasise action and experiential learning, and class sessions are lively. Young entrepreneurs are involved as role models, and students on the KBS Master's in International Entrepreneurship Management programme also get involved, which is a good experience for all concerned. Most of the programme is located in the school, but the students also come in regularly to the Enterprise Centre in the KBS. This allows them to access the Bloomberg Trading Floor, and gets them used to the idea of a university as a place that they can easily come to and learn.

What happened

Our aim with both programmes is to encourage students to see university life as an option, as a reason to stay in school. This is particularly overt in CAA where the material is not restricted to business or innovation. The delivery of the programmes brought practical logistical challenges. The CAA students, for instance, coming in to KBS in the evening after school needed a meal. Because ICE was largely delivered in the students' own school, there were also logistical issues: for example, creating space in the timetable for longer blocks of work, having flexibility for guest speakers, adjusting the language and tone of creativity and innovation material for the age group.

The delivery of the ICE programme also brought challenges, particularly for the teachers who had worked in a far more structured environment before. They moved from delivering state-mandated curriculum to becoming facilitators of a very dynamic learning process, sometimes surrendering accountability and decision-making to student learners. The teachers were faced with the challenge of moving to transformative teaching and delivery approaches extending them from their typical role of a conveyor of knowledge to a networker, facilitator, coach, mentor and challenger, and they responded to these challenges very powerfully. While students largely exhibited considerable enthusiasm for this structured flexibility, there were also some signs of anxiety in the face of a change in didactic format, which extended both teachers and students beyond their comfort zones. These issues underline the importance of training and mentoring for secondary teachers involved in such novel delivery.

What next?

These two programmes were very successful in separate ways. In CAA, we performed an entry and exit survey of each class, and the results are striking. Asked at the beginning of the programme whether or not they would like to attend university after school, only 20% responded yes. At the end of the programme, this had risen to 70%.

The feedback from the teachers and students on ICE was also extremely positive, with students highlighting their increased confidence and self-knowledge. Both students and teachers reported that the skills acquired on the ICE programme transferred easily to other subjects. The ultimate success of this pilot programme came when it was approved by the National Department of Education and is now a recognised state exam programme. Coláiste Chiaráin became the first school in Ireland to implement the new three-year junior cycle programme, under National Council for Curriculum and Assessment guidelines. A new pilot ICE programme is being developed for the senior cycle of secondary school, targeting students aged 16 to 18. Ultimately, this may be accredited for the state exams in a similar way to the junior ICE programme.

Future work on CAA will involve creating learning packs for students to bring back to their schools, and also establishing workshops for parents to attend while their children gain the benefits of the CAA programme. These may include adult literacy and financial literacy skills. In particular, and subject to resources becoming available, the programme will expand not just to more DEIS schools, but to more DEIS children. One of the features of the Limerick regeneration policy is the displacement of previously tightly knit communities into other areas. The issues which may have existed do not disappear once the family has moved, however, although this does make it much harder for the CAA programme to target these families. Working through existing school completion and school liaison programmes, it should be possible to identify these students.

The development phase of both of these programmes was intensive in terms of time and expenditure, but the outcomes are clearly positive. They meet the challenge of collaborating with second-level schools to address a societal challenge, and address a key action in the School's 2013–2016 Strategic Plan to 'Increase collaboration with local schools and ensure greater access by students from a variety of social backgrounds'. They help the School to connect with our stakeholders in a meaningful way. They also align well with principles 5 and 6 of PRME: partnership and dialogue to address issues of social sustainability. For the students, we hope they break down some barriers and help them to see the unlimited potential of their own talent.

References

Hourigan, N. (2011) *Understanding Limerick: Social Exclusion and Change* (Cork, Ireland: Cork University Press).

Humphreys, E., D. McCafferty and A. Higgins (2012) *How Are Our Kids?* (Report; Limerick: Limerick Regeneration Agencies; Dublin: Atlantic Philanthropies).

Healion, E. (2013) *Perceived Effects of an Academic Enrichment Programme for Potentially Gifted Students from a Socio-economic Disadvantaged Area Using Critical Action Research* (PhD thesis; Dublin: Dublin City University).

Smyth, E. (1999) 'Educational Inequalities among School Leavers in Ireland 1979–1994', Economic and Social Review 30.3 (1999): 267-284.

O'Connell, P.J., S. McCoy and D. Clancy (2006) 'Who Went to College? Socio-economic Inequality in Entry to Higher Education in the Republic of Ireland in 2004', *Higher Education Quarterly* 60.4: 312-32.

McCoy, S., D. Byrne, P.J. O'Connell, E. Kelly and C. Doherty (2010) *Hidden Disadvantage? A Study on the Low Participation in Higher Education by the Non-manual Group*. NUI Maynooth Working Paper. Available online at http://eprints.nuim.ie/4366/1/DB_Hidden_Disadvantage.pdf

9 *Using university space to create socioeconomic impact*

Alec Wersun, Nathan Tagg and Susan Grant

Glasgow Caledonian University

Glasgow, Scotland

Introduction

Glasgow Caledonian University's (GCU) motto and guiding principle is 'For the Common Good'. To reflect this, the university is committed to using its skills, knowledge and facilities to make a positive contribution to the well-being of the communities it serves at home and overseas. The primary means of delivering on this commitment are engagement in dialogue and partnership with stakeholders in the community, reflecting two of the six principles of responsible management education (PRME). Extensive dialogue with stakeholder groups informs the design of teaching degrees, shapes the university's research agenda, and leads to the development of collaborative programmes that improve the economic and social well-being of those in the community—something that is intrinsic to the university's mission of working for the 'Common Good'.[1]

---

1   For more about the university's approach to PRME please see the GCU website, 'PRME', www.gcu.ac.uk/prme/, accessed 27 June 2014.

Challenge

This case presents an example of a collaborative community effort, the aim of which is to raise education and life aspirations of families from areas with above average levels of social and economic deprivation. The context for this work can be summarised as follows:

- 20% of Scottish entrants to GCU come from the lowest quintile of multiple deprivation, compared with a sector average of 12%
- 97% of GCU students come from state schools, compared with the local average of 88%
- 73% of GCU undergraduates are the first in their family to attend university

What we did

Following a period of wide consultation with stakeholders in the city of Glasgow, GCU established the 'Caledonian Club' in 2008 as a vehicle to widen access to higher education from communities with high levels of deprivation. Adopting a 'cluster' model that includes a nursery, primary and secondary school, the Caledonian Club works with five Glasgow communities with traditionally low levels of onward transition from school to higher education. The Caledonian Club actively engages with the local communities in championing the importance of education and lifelong learning among pupils and families, thereby contributing to generational change in social inclusion and the economic and social sustainability of communities.

To give context to the figures shown in Table 1 and to accurately represent the challenges faced within the Club's communities, the

percentage of Scottish school-leavers progressing to higher education in Scotland sits at 36%; within Glasgow the progression rate
is 28%, while the average for the Caledonian Club's five secondary
schools is significantly lower at just 17.2%.

TABLE 1 Caledonian Club participating schools

School	HE progression (%)
All Saints Secondary	24
Springburn Academy	21
Drumchapel High	10
Whitehill Secondary	21
St Margaret Mary's	10
Average	17.2

Source: Education Scotland's Scottish Schools online database, www.educationscotland.gov.uk/scot
tishschoolsonline/index.asp, accessed 27 June 2014

The Club has eight core activities:

- Nursery Campus Visit: a two-part preschool activity (age 4)
- Primary Digital Book project 2 (age 6).
- Primary 5 University Day Animation project (age 9)
- S1 Introduction to student life project (age 12)
- S3 'Think Ahead' project (age 14)
- S6 Professor's Challenge (age 16–17)
- S6 Shadowing (age 16–17)
- S6 Mentoring project (age 17)

Sustainability of the Caledonian Club is reflected in cumulative
membership numbers, which recently stood at approximately
5,300 pupils and 2,000 parents. As an example of a year's activity
levels, across the academic year of 2011–12, and within the Club's
core activities, Table 2 shows the levels of engagement with pupils
and parents.

TABLE 2 Levels of community engagement in the Caledonian Club, 2011–2012

Project	Pupils	Parents
Nursery	181	93
Nursery Graduation	36	87
Primary 2	174	49
P5 Animation	164	74
S1 Project	477	16
S4 Summer Project	87	20
S5/6 Professors Challenge	234	0
S6 Shadowing	169	0
S6 Mentoring	48	0
Projects total	1570	339

Following further consultation with other GCU stakeholders, the Club partnered with computer giant Dell in 2011 on one of their projects. The **S6 Professor's Challenge** comprises an annual team-building workshop in school followed by a two-day campus visit, which involves pupils working on a marketing challenge set by a GCU business partner. Each team has sub-teams working on IT, product and graphic design, research and marketing, and sub-teams consult experts in the relevant areas. All pupils take part in a pitching workshop and spend time with a drama leader to work on their presentation. They then pitch to a judging panel in front of an audience of their peers, teachers, GCU staff and Dell representatives.

It is this partnership with Dell that has really enhanced the GCU Professor's Challenge because it is bringing real-life business problems to pupils, helping pupils to develop entrepreneurial thinking and action, while making business expertise available to them. Dell is a global company with a Scottish head office on GCU's doorstep in the east end of Glasgow. While the company has an active corporate social responsibility policy, which includes some local school engagement, it does not have the long-established relationships with schools, nor the type of infrastructure required for deep school engagement enjoyed by GCU. This is what GCU brings to Dell. While 'doing good', the project offers Dell access to the ideas and views of a young target consumer group of pupils (age 16–17) and university students. These factors combine to make great sense for Dell to partner with GCU in a community engagement project.

What happened

The Caledonian Club project is a manifestation of GCU's mission to work for the common good. Involvement of an increasing number of staff and students in the Club's activities reflects the energy and commitment of the GCU community to use management education to bring about positive change, to be a force for good, and to contribute to economic and social sustainability.

Typical of stakeholder feedback on the Caledonian Club is the following statement:

> This project has increased the confidence of pupils, particularly ones that do not normally present (in public). All pupils have developed excellent communication and team working skills, and learned to work to deadlines. It has been a great pleasure seeing pupils out with the classroom and interacting well with others in a new environment.

After one of the projects, one of the pupils commented that 'It's been a hard challenge and because it's a big company like Dell, it's going to mean something to them. They are putting a lot of hope in us so it gives us a big responsibility'.

Dell delivers a real-life business problem, which thoroughly engages and enthuses senior pupils and mentors. Dell experts provide guidance, GCU staff and students act as mentors. Combined with access to excellent resources on campus, the project provides young people with unforgettable and worthwhile experiences both for their final year at school and beyond. Winners of the challenge each receive a tablet computer from Dell. Pupils from the short-listed teams are invited to Dell for a site visit and for an employability skills session. Pupils also put their new-found presentation skills and confidence into practice and make a presentation to the wider Dell management board on their experience.

Some of the pupils who participated in the Dell Challenge have gone on to become GCU students, or gone to other places of higher education. Caledonian Club mentors go back to their old schools to *inspire* more pupils to aim for higher education. Dell started working with the Club in 2011 and completed its third business challenge for this project in 2013 due to the success of the project for pupils, students and Dell employees.[2]

What next?

The Caledonian Club model of community partnership and engagement is being introduced in London and New York, where GCU has recently opened satellite campuses. In Glasgow and London the model is being complemented by work carried out as a member of Business in the Community[3] and Scottish Business in the Community[4]—the UK's largest corporate responsibility organisation. This has resulted in the recent launch of two new three-year strategic partnerships with schools in Glasgow and Dagenham, using BITC's 'Business Class' programme framework. Business Class provides a systematic and proven framework for developing partnerships with schools, rooted in long-term, strategic support and collaborative action. The authors plan to keep the PRME community informed of the impact that such education-based collaborations can have across whole communities.

2   For more information see the S6 Challenge video on the GCU website, www.gcu.ac.uk/caledonianclub/activities/secondary/s5-6/s6challenge video/, accessed 27 June 2014.
3   www.bitc.org.uk, accessed 27 June 2014.
4   www.sbcscot.com/, accessed 27 June 2014.

Role of principles: PRME

The United Nations PRME have challenged businesses and universities to contribute to poverty alleviation and work with communities on issues of economic and social sustainability. This project does just that by drawing on Principles Five and Six of PRME, the principles of partnership and dialogue. In this case, extensive dialogue with community and business leaders has led to the design and implementation of a multi-stakeholder project that reflects the university's mission of working for the common good. PRME 5 and 6 have:

- Inspired the university to work with business and community leaders to tackle poverty
- Used educational innovation to address the challenge of low aspiration levels in communities of multiple deprivation
- Had an impact on the improvement of social mobility and sustainability

10 Engaging Hertfordshire Business School students with the local community

Jana Filosof

Hertfordshire Business School

Hatfield, England

Introduction

Hertfordshire Business School is one of the largest schools in the University of Hertfordshire with over 4,000 students. It offers a range of undergraduate and postgraduate courses in the fields of business and management, human resources, marketing, accounting and finance, economics, information systems, management sciences and tourism, and three doctoral programmes (PhD, DBA and DMan). Before HBS became a PRME signatory in 2011, the concept of responsibility had already been embedded in our learning and teaching, research and engagement with stakeholders. Joining PRME has prompted us to take a more strategic and systematic approach to delivering responsible education. A role of a PRME champion had synergies with the work of the Social Enterprise Unit. That champion is a dedicated promoter and coordinator for the range of responsible education activities in HBS, and a valuable resource for those colleagues interested in further engagement with the Principles. The principles of PRME also have a strategic fit with the University of Hertfordshire Graduate Attributes, especially the attribute of Social Responsibility.

Challenge

The UN PRME principles are embedded into all management areas in HBS. Significant focus has been placed across a number of undergraduate and postgraduate modules directly on ethics and corporate social responsibility in large organisations. This has also prompted the opportunity to develop detailed student discussions in tutorials. Students are typically introduced to the key literatures and current debates in modules. Drawing on competing perspectives they learn how to evaluate the good and bad practices of contemporary business from a critical and informed position. This leaves, however, several areas less explored: for example, how those theories and models are translated in a particular organisation; how individual participants contribute to the emergence of ethics in an organisation; and how we, as a major stakeholder in Hertfordshire, can contribute to the local community.

What we did

We designed two modules, one postgraduate and one undergraduate, that require students to volunteer in the local community, as part of the module assessment strategy, in order to gain a better understanding of their topic of study. We identified several benefits to students in taking the experiential learning approach:

- Engaging students with the local community
- Developing greater appreciation of the topic through experiential learning
- Enhancing innovative learning and teaching strategies

We also identified several challenges of this method:

- Allocating the appropriate weighing to the volunteering element in the assessment

- Fostering students' ability to find a suitable volunteering opportunity to both enhance their learning and to contribute to the local community

The former challenge was addressed by working closely with the University of Hertfordshire Learning and Teaching Institute and the external examiners. The Social Enterprise Unit was instrumental in addressing the latter. Through the work of the Unit, HBS has developed partnerships with many organisations in the third sector. We approached managers in those organisations and explained the nature of each module. Our close relationships with those organisations allowed us to develop several possible volunteering opportunities for each organisation. We asked the managers whether they would be happy to support the student volunteers. The list of volunteering opportunities for each module was then posted on the modules' websites.

In addition, the students were encouraged to approach the Student Union, and to explore their own interests in obtaining voluntary placements. To ensure that the placement was indeed appropriate for the module all placements have to be approved by the module leader.

The short discussion below demonstrates how this approach was translated on two very different modules.

Understanding challenges in the third sector

The module was developed in order to expose more HBS undergraduate students to the growing third sector.[1] This sector is traditionally not the focus of the academic curricula of business schools (by definition, the business of the business schools is business).

---

[1]   The 'third sector' is a relatively new title for activity that has a long tradition in the UK and at its most basic is a term for defining activity that falls outside of the public and private sector (Hopkins 2010).

However, the contribution of the third sector to the economy and society is significant (approximately 2.4% of GDP; Ainsworth 2013) and the 'third sector workforce is growing and professionalising' (Hopkins 2010: 4). The sector is different from the public and private sectors, and traditional frameworks that have been developed for managing the private and public sectors cannot be simply translated into the third sector.

The module aims to equip the students with an in-depth understanding of the challenges the managers in the third sector face. In addition to the theoretical part of the module that is covered in the lectures, the students are required to volunteer for 50 hours in a third sector organisation and to discuss the applicability and the relevance of theory with the manager in that organisation. These discussions, the students' experiences and readings will feed into tutorials and those in turn, will feed the discussions. The learning on the module, therefore, is an iterative process, encompassing both in-class and experiential learning.

This is an optional module, and we were pleasantly surprised that many students chose this module in the first year of delivery, despite the requirement of 50 hours of additional out-of-class work; 32 volunteered in charities and other non-for-profit organisations and 5 in social enterprises. The students' initial reaction to the module design was overwhelmingly that of surprise and bewilderment. For most of them it was the first time they had encountered the request for volunteering as an integral part of the module. However, the lectures addressing the theory and the seminar discussions reflecting on what was happening in their organisations allowed the students to fully appreciate this pedagogical approach. As one student reflected,

> This week in lectures we learned about the financing of the third sector and social and ethical capital. On the day of my placement I sat with my supervisor/manager to discuss these topics with her, and come down (sic) to an understanding of how important these topics were, within the organisation.

The contribution of the module to the students' learning and the community was noticeable. The students gained appreciation of the third sector by practically engaging with the organisation:

> I am privileged to have taken part in this placement, it was very beneficial to me as I learned a lot from applying what I had learnt and read about, into real life situations. From working with Real Drama I gained an understanding of how hard it is to be a Third Sector Organisation within the UK.

This also enhanced their employability by developing their skills and competences and providing them with some work experience. We also received positive comments from the employers about the impact of the students on their organisations. This impact and contribution are also evident from the fact that all organisations providing placements for our students in 2012–13 have asked to be part of this project in the current academic year.

What happened

The module design encourages the student to take a reflective approach to their understanding of leadership. The module is assessed by reflective narratives, discussing the students' experience of leading and being led, managing and being managed. This assessment strategy provided an opportunity to introduce an assignment that encourages more engagement of the HBS students with the community.

The brief is simple. The students are required to form small groups and design and deliver an 8-hour community project. They then have to submit an individual essay reflecting on the entire process, focusing on issues of leadership, group dynamics and power relations.

Although the internal and the external examiners highly praised this 'innovative assessment design', it has initially been met with scepticism and uncertainty from students. The comments like 'what does community work have to do with leadership?', and 'we don't have time for this', have arisen repeatedly since the introduction of this component. In reflecting on their experience and writing their narratives the students come to understand the importance of the project to their learning '(t)he community project (planting trees for the Woodland Trust), which at one stage, I thought was a waste of our time, actually has had a considerable impact on me and on my learning journey', and their development as leaders and followers: 'I found that the community group experience extremely positive and has given me further insight into my own strengths and weaknesses within group and social activities'. Furthermore, they come to appreciate leadership and ethics as arising in continuous interaction between people '(i)t is my belief that the leadership was shifting at different times and was being transferred around the group members at different points during the community projects'. They also find taking part in supporting their community gratifying: 'planning and undertaking this group task was a refreshing and rewarding experience'. The photos present just one example of how a project was received by its beneficiaries.

IMAGE 1 **The completed project**

IMAGE 2 A thank-you card presented by the children

This case study is an example of how engaging with PRME impacted our design of teaching and learning, and led us to develop modules which assist us in engaging our students with the principles of responsible management.

The principles that are specifically addressed in this case study are Purpose, Values, Method and Dialogue.

References

Ainsworth, D. (2013) 'Sector's Contribution to the Economy "Could Be Four Times Larger than Thought"', Third Sector Online, 20 March 2013, www.thirdsector .co.uk/Finance/article/1175239/sectors-contribution-economy-could-four-times-larger-thought/, accessed 12 January 2014.

Hopkins, L. (2010) Mapping the Third Sector: A Context for Social Leadership (Clore Social Leadership Programme; London: The Work Foundation).

Part C

Developing programmes in research and learning and teaching

11 *Not everything in textbooks is true: Teaching discourse analysis to undergraduate business students*

Tina Bass

Coventry University Business School

Coventry, England

Introduction

Coventry University adopted the United Nations' Principles for Responsible Management in 2007 and, more recently, the Business School has taken up the challenge to embed these important principles throughout their course offerings in order to provide the very best education for future business leaders. 'Managing Business Responsibly' is a final-year, undergraduate module which was created two years ago and which grew partly out of some of my previous teaching. This is an optional module for which students are clamouring to sign up as it is one of the few that has no examination and is assessed wholly on coursework. They very quickly realise that it is not a soft option. The module poses a series of critical challenges to students and in the first few weeks many find it uncomfortable as the theories drawn upon are not those generally found within a business course. Students are encouraged to consider both their individual values and how these may or may not be reflected at a corporate level: What kind of manager do they ultimately want to be? And how do they become?

Challenge

As an undergraduate I was inspired by the writings of E.F. Schumacher and the challenges posed to capitalism with his concepts of 'enoughness' and 'Buddhist Economics'. Around the same time I was also introduced to Paolo Freire's writings and 25 years later I am still thinking about the implications of his discussions of the emancipatory potential of education and the dangers of education that purports to be neutral while perpetuating hidden political agendas. Since the financial crisis of 2007/8 along with the preceding business failures of Enron *et al.* there have been an increasing number of academics who have made a connection between the world of business and business teaching. They have pointed to a managerialist/neo-liberal ideology prevailing in business schools and a lack of ethics among both business students and business school academics. While not all of these writers are drawing from empirical evidence, there are certainly strong and persuasive arguments that if you repeatedly teach from a particular frame of reference, such as neo-liberalism, it becomes very difficult to conceive of a world that is organised in any other way. For students educated within a narrow ideology this means that they potentially leave university armed with a limited range of language with which to, borrowing Freire's words, name the world.

What we did

Within the module students are invited to think of themselves as agents of change in the broadest sense and to carefully consider those aspects of their current or future organisations that they might be able to influence. The rational model of decision-making is held up for particular scrutiny and consideration is given to how it may effectively be supplemented by non-traditional methods. Social constructionist theory features in the first few weeks and conversation patterns, narratives, discourses and storytelling are all explored as potential tools for business students who aspire to become responsible managers.

Discourse analysis in particular has proven to be a useful and flexible means for encouraging students to critique the models and theories that they have been taught. In order to guard against plagiarism, and possibly because I enjoy it, I literally rip several pages from a strategy textbook and present the scanned version to the students as the basis for their first assessed piece of work. Reactions to this assessment are quite often nervousness and uncertainty. For some of the students the act of challenging something from a textbook written by someone that they consider to be much cleverer than themselves is both disturbing and disorienting. In order to teach students how to approach the text I start with a simple discourse analysis of an advertising image in which a scantily dressed woman is feeding a man some ice-cream. Students are asked to raise their hands if they see the woman as occupying a dominant role (she is seated higher than the man and has control of the ice-cream), a subservient role or a maternal one. Most classes have a mixture of responses which is a perfect introduction to the notion of multiple truths. We all take something from the image but we also bring our discourses to it. Our culture and experiences shape what we see in the picture and there is no single truth that can be taken from the image. There is also little point in arguing with others that our truth is clearly better/more obvious/ more rational than theirs. Then we move on to examine potential discourses in a small piece of text which generally the students find much more difficult to grasp.

What happened

The module team have to work extremely hard to manage student anxiety around this coursework and have to repeatedly stress that discourse analysis is an invaluable critical thinking tool. I believe that it *is* extremely useful but presenting it in this way also helps the students to view the approach as a legitimate one and not as something odd that they can then disengage from. They are cautioned against looking too widely for definitions of discourses and discourse analysis as the differing uses of the term in different disciplines can be highly confusing. Vivien Burr's definition in *Social Constructionism* is the one most frequently used within this context alongside a small selection of web links and some pages from *Management and Organization* by Linstead, Fulop and Lilley. I also skip lightly over some of Foucault's work during one of the lecture sessions. Students are not expected to become experts in this area but to engage with the activity and to begin to appreciate the possibility of a world of multiple truths with as many ways of understanding as there are people in it.

This is not an easy transition for the students but it also presents some challenges for the teaching staff too. There are ethical issues that have to be managed as students view their final year of study as high risk and teaching something entirely new puts pressures on them that academic staff need to appreciate and manage. As an academic operating within a business school I am also constantly being made aware of the need to consider and address student satisfaction. The National Student Survey (taken by final year undergraduates) has an impact on the way that we can advertise our courses and directly affects how positively we are viewed by the general public. More directly personally, as an academic working within a business school, if my students express dissatisfaction with my teaching this may have an impact on any review of my performance and affect my potential for progression.

What next?

I believe that those business undergraduates who engage with discourse analysis benefit enormously from the experience. Not only does discourse analysis expand their vocabulary and understanding of the world it can also help them to appreciate the difference between being genuinely open and respectful of the views of others and simply saying that they are. By the time the module draws to a close, students regularly approach me to say 'thank you' for the experience. There are also regular comments to suggest that they would have liked to learn about discourses much earlier as they can see the benefits in other coursework. Some even comment on how useful they will find it in terms of understanding and challenging organisational culture and language. I am satisfied that despite the struggles for the academics and students, learning about discourses and discourse analysis helps young people who will soon be moving into graduate positions to be a little more at ease in a complex and uncertain world.

References

Burr, V. 2003: Social Constructionism (second edition). London: Routledge

Linstead, S., Fulop E. and Lilley, S. 2009: Management and Organization - a critical text (second edition). London: Palgrave Macmillan.

12 *Education for sustainable development at the School of Management, University of Bradford*

Kyoko Fukukawa

Bradford University School of Management

Bradford, England

Introduction

The School of Management at University of Bradford became a UN PRME signatory in 2010, following participation in a major university-wide project to implement Education for Sustainable Development (ESD). The organisational impact of this project and its legacy brings to the fore a number of points of interest for those looking to meet the challenges of and/or sustain success in implementing the Principles for Responsible Management Education (PRME).

PRME's core principles of raising students' capabilities, embedding social responsibility in the curriculum, designing effective learning experiences, understanding and partnering with businesses, as well as maintaining ongoing dialogue with stakeholder groups, were all at the heart of the University of Bradford's Eco-versity project, which ran from 2007 to 2010. The project was funded by the UK's central state funding body, Higher Education Funding Council for England (Hefce), with a grant of £3.1 million to help position the university as a centre of excellence for sustainability education and research. A proportion of the funding was allocated to six schools across the university, including the Business School, for the embedding of ESD into the formal curriculum.

The university's aim for this element of the project was to develop discipline-led, student-relevant and *locally* meaningful ESD developments. Thus, while the project was initiated by the university's senior administration, and underpinned by three years of financial support, there was equally a bottom-up approach critical to its ambitions.

Challenge

In the wake of the financial crisis, business schools can be said to have come under criticism for having too narrowly educated executives with curricula focused on process efficiencies and profit maximisation, against which, it is argued, curricula need to consider more ethical approaches to business and offer greater focus on sustainability. The School of Management at the University of Bradford sought to bring about change through a consultative process, with the aim to make ESD an explicit dimension of existing and emergent curricula. Of course, within the complex organisational structure of a university, the challenge is inevitably to find suitable means to bring about significant and lasting change. Attuned to such difficulties, Beer and Eisenstat's (1996) action-based research framework identifies three key principles of effective change: that it should be systemic, should encourage the 'open discussion of barriers', and should develop a partnership with all relevant stakeholders. It is through the lens of these principles that the development of ESD at Bradford's School of Management can be understood.

What we did

The change process was strategic in that ESD was identified by both the University *and* the School as part of their vision and mission, and integral to the growth and 'competitive' positioning of the institution. However, at School-level there were three 'agents' critical to the formalisation of ESD within the School of Management: ESD champions, or 'Academic Pioneers'; the Associate Dean for Learning and Teaching; and an ESD Working Group. The Academic Pioneer role was undertaken by established academics, in possession of current and regular experience of face-to-face delivery of teaching. Their task was to liaise with colleagues throughout the School to gain an in-depth picture of current provision and to champion the embedding of ESD across the curriculum. Project members contributed to facilitating a school-wide consultation (on pedagogical and operational issues) and formulating policies. Throughout its duration and at its summation, the working group and senior management of the School and University measured the project against a 'Deliverables Matrix'. The 'Deliverables Matrix' was developed by the Academic Pioneers (in consultation with the ESD working group), aligning University and School aims with roles of responsibility and outputs or actions. Through this mechanism, the ESD project was able to assess its impact in a number of specified ways.

Academic Pioneers conducted an audit of ESD practices within the School of Management, along with content analysis of all programme and module documentation. Information was also gained through staff email surveys and semi-structured interviews. The interview process helped clarify how curriculum development might proceed and various measures were taken in an attempt to embed ESD further within the School. A working group was established to develop policy and consider pedagogical approaches to ESD implementation. In addition, various opportunities were created for stakeholder partnerships, which included a seminar series with external speakers, working with alumni, supporting researchers interested in ESD from other institutions, and communicating with professional and accreditation bodies such as AACSB (Association to Advance Collegiate Schools of Business) and PRME. Agreement over the place and purpose of ESD within the School and its curriculum was ultimately achieved because of the negotiated understanding of ESD developed through working with a wide cross-section of academic staff.

What happened

Beer and Eisenstat's (1996) three principles of effective change help explain the combination of approaches critical to ensuring the uptake of ESD. Of these, it is the second principle, **open discussion of barriers**, that appeared most significant in guiding change. Academic Pioneers and their engagement with faculty through interviews, the working group and in the School-wide consultation provided opportunities for stakeholders to work through their concerns with ESD and its implementation. Dialogue provided the means for faculty to develop their own sense of the place of ESD in their practice. The exact nature of ESD was, within the frameworks outlined by the institution, individually determined, and faculty came to adjust their practices in response to the initiative. This suggests that the *open discussion of barriers* was critical in developing the third principle, **partnership among stakeholders**, although the levels of partnership were limited (and hence overall agreement on specific ESD requirements was not required).

TABLE 1 Education for sustainable development as a process of change

Change stage	Initiation	Implementation	Integration
Impacts through	Institution	Change agents	Individual sense-making
Level of focus	University	School (as organisational unit)	Faculty (as individuals)
Key actors	Senior management (change sponsors)	Academic Pioneers (change agents)	Academic staff (change recipients)

Source: this table is adapted from a full account of this case study in Fukukawa *et al.* 2013

The role of Academic Pioneers was also critical in supporting Beer and Eisenstat's (1996) first principle, **that the change process was systematic**. This occurred through engagement with staff to coordinate change across the School, and which was focused on identifying a fit between outcomes at the School level and the University strategy for ESD. Taken together, the process of the change needs to be understood in different ways, as the perspective, focus and key drivers shift. Table 1 schematises three such instances, labelled as three change stages, **initiation**, **implementation** and **integration**, and identifies the key aspects of each. The position, level and perspective of the actors in relation to the change affect how it is enacted, perceived and applied. Here the process of ESD implementation is explained and accommodated very differently depending on whether you are the instigator of the change (senior management), its agent (Academic Pioneers), or recipients (academic staff). However, these differences should not be perceived as elements of the process itself. Change did not occur in a linear fashion, proceeding through these perspectives as stages, but rather represents a set of varying and interdependent forces at work.

What next?

The above account of differing characteristics of initiation, implementation and integration within the experience of the development of ESD can potentially act as a framework to guide others seeking to develop ESD in their own institutions. It is significant that the majority of the actions for change lie at the implementation stage. Success here came from a largely devolved approach to change. With a clear purpose and agenda set by the University, change agents at the School level had the responsibility for enacting and implementing ESD in ways appropriate to their contexts. This led to significant adaption of the policy to suit the School's own educational agenda.

A fuller account of this case study, with a particular focus on the theory and practice of organisational change, can be read in the paper titled 'Sustainable Change: Education for Sustainable Development in the Business School' (Fukukawa *et al.* 2013). The phrase 'sustainable change' is used to refer to the introduction and embedding of the principles of sustainability at the School of Management. Yet, importantly, while the study offers a positive account of the integration of ESD, an ongoing concern is that individual instances of engagement with ESD may remain superficial, only paying lip service to institutional directives. Thus, 'sustainable change' is also meant to describe a process of implementation that is itself sustainable. The role of Academic Pioneers in facilitating discussion and reflection on ESD was regarded as significant in affecting change, affording individual academics a deliberative space to negotiate the impact of ESD on their own practice, helping to accommodate their own values and integrity. However, it is also vital that interest is maintained by senior managers, who, structurally, are the key enablers of the whole process, ensuring the aims and ambitions are built into, as well as steered by, strategic planning and resource allocation. Effective change is best conceptualised as a collaborative process, and in this vein ESD should itself be ongoing and long term if its impact is to be judged truly successful. It is in this regard that a key outcome of the project has been the establishment of the role of PRME Lead within the School, a role undertaken by an academic member of staff, whose work—in the fashion of Academic Pioneer—is to continually inquire into whether the integration and synthesis put into process by the ESD project is indeed still in place.

References

Beer, M., and R.A. Eisenstat (1996) 'Developing an Organization Capable of Implementing Strategy and Learning', *Human Relations* 49: 597-619.

Fukukawa, K., D. Spicer, S.A. Burrows and J. Fairbrass (2013) 'Sustainable Change: Education for Sustainable Development in the Business School', *Journal of Corporate Citizenship* 49: 71-99.

13 Hairdressers and sustainability: Showing how our research impacts society

Denise Baden

School of Management, University of Southampton

Southampton, England

Introduction

The School of Management, University of Southampton signed up to the UN-backed Principles for Responsible Management Education in 2009 and have found them to be a useful framework under which to integrate issues of sustainability, ethics and responsibility into our activities. In this case study I present details of an ongoing research project which addresses Principle 4, **Research**: 'We will engage in conceptual and empirical research that advances our understanding about the role, dynamics, and impact of corporations in the creation of sustainable social, environmental and economic value'.

Academia is often accused of focusing too much on theory and not doing enough to address real world challenges. I believe that this criticism applies equally to business/management schools, and so was very keen that our research engaged directly and effectively with the business sector to help them meet the challenges of sustainable development.

Challenge

The challenges of sustainable development are becoming increasingly urgent, with the UK, like many other nations, struggling to meet its carbon-reduction targets, reduce waste, pollution, and energy and water consumption. Yet although the challenges presented by sustainable development are broadly accepted, resource use increases unabated. It is increasingly acknowledged that while technical solutions may play a part, a key issue is behaviour change. In response to this there has been a plethora of studies into how behaviour change can be enabled, predominantly from psychological and sociological perspectives. This has resulted in a substantial body of knowledge into the factors that drive behaviour change and how they can be manipulated to achieve desired social goals. However, we wanted to do more than add to theory, and instead wanted to draw on this body of knowledge to design effective business interventions.

Many large companies are now demonstrating increased sustainability awareness and environmental policies, in part because of the requirements of new regulations such as the Carbon Reduction Commitment, and also because of their brand exposure. However behaviour at the level of small companies and individuals has been slower to change. This is a problem as SMEs are an important part of the economy, accounting for 99% of European enterprises, and 67% of total employment (Wymenga *et al.*, 2012). SMEs are considered to be the largest contributors to pollution, carbon dioxide emissions and commercial waste (Williamson *et al.*, 2006). It is therefore crucial to engage SMEs in making the transition to a more sustainable economy. The hair and beauty sector comprises mostly SMEs and forms 5% of UK GDP (HABIA 2012). The sector involves very high energy use, water use and toxic chemicals, yet pilot research (Baden 2010) shows minimal awareness of environmental issues.

Targeting hairdressers to increase their motivation, knowledge and ability to engage in more pro-environmental behaviours can thus make an important contribution to sustainability. In addition, and potentially more importantly, targeting hairdressers to influence their clients to adopt more sustainable practices (e.g. washing less often, washing just once, blow drying less, using organic products etc.) allows a greater impact towards less resource-intensive practices across the general population.

Social psychological research and research into behaviour change indicate that a key driver of behaviour is social norms (Cialdini 2003). However even when people are aware of what they should do (injunctive norms) a stronger driver of behaviour is descriptive norms, or what everyone else is doing (Oceja and Berenguer 2009). Therefore, attempts to change behaviour need to take into account social norms. Pro-environmental behaviours can be seen as social innovations as they require a change in behaviour. Diffusion theory indicates that innovations spread through a social network faster if they are promoted by those who are either part of many diverse networks, or are seen as trusted and relevant sources of information; that is, 'catalytic individuals'. Hairdressers fulfil both these criteria as hairdressers talk to more people as part of their work than most other occupations, and thus are part of many social networks. In addition, hairdressers will be seen as relatively knowledgeable in the area of hair care.

Our objectives therefore fell into two main areas: increasing environmental sustainability in the hairdressing sector and exploring the role of hairdressers as diffusers of social norms relating to pro-environmental behaviour.

What we did

The project took the form of action research, with the methodology informed by the literature on community-based social marketing (McKenzie-Mohr 2000). This approach identifies the barriers to the activity to be promoted, and draws on the literature on behaviour change to devise interventions to overcome such barriers. Barriers to pro-environmental behaviours (PEBs) emerging from our pilot study with hairdressers (Baden 2010) were lack of awareness and insufficient motivation, in part due to lack of self-efficacy in the domain of pro-environmental behaviours. The strategy adopted to overcome these barriers was to invite hairdressers to an event—the Green Salon Makeover—to raise awareness of PEBs in their work and encourage them to come up with their own ideas to reduce environmental impacts. This was followed three months later by a follow-up event to share information on what worked and to gain environmental certification.[1]

This strategy was informed by discussions with hairdressers and hairdressing bodies, and by the social psychology motivational literature (Jackson, 2005) in order to maximise the participants' motivation to adopt PEBs. For example, based on the Theory of Planned Behaviour (Ajzen, 1985), we used an inspirational speaker to inform hairdressers about the challenges of sustainability, thus increasing their knowledge and awareness of the issues and creating positive attitudes towards adopting more sustainable practices. The speaker drew on many examples of business to highlight how many were addressing these challenges. A key point made was that businesses were not waiting for their customers to ask for sustainable products, but assumed their customers expected them to care without being asked and were taking the lead. The removal of patio heaters from B&Q's product range and their sourcing of wood solely from FSC-certified forests were given as an example. This point 'normed' the idea that businesses are ahead of their customers on sustainability issues. This was important as our pilot study indicated that few hairdressers reported that customers ask them about environmental issues. The speaker also increased self-efficacy by giving many examples of how businesses were adopting more sustainable practices; choosing cases where the relevant issues (e.g. choice of what products to sell) were easily transferable to the hairdressing sector. By giving examples of successful businesses and also many small businesses, hairdressers gained

---

1   The follow-up event was hosted in conjunction with 'Steps Towards Environmental Management', a new environmental certificate designed for small business.

knowledge of how to be sustainable thus creating positive control beliefs that more sustainable practices were possible.

Before the Green Salon Makeover, hairdressers were given a collection box and batch of mini-surveys and asked to request their customers to complete the survey before leaving the salon. The survey was brief to encourage a high response, with four questions:

- Does the customer consider environmental issues in relation to hair-care such as energy use in drying/styling hair, water consumption or toxicity of hair-care products?
- Was there any indication of such issues being considered in their visit to the hairdresser?
- Are practices relating to hair-care at home influenced by experiences at the hairdresser e.g. in terms of how long to dry/rinse hair, what hair products to use etc.?
- Would customers like hairdressers to consider such issues?

What happened

The intervention was successful: interview and survey data from the hairdressers indicated positive intentions to adopt more sustainable practices within their salons and pass them on to their customers. The customer survey (N=776) confirms this: customers surveyed after their hairdresser attended the Green Salon Makeover intervention were significantly more likely to report that environmental issues had been considered in their salon visit and that they themselves would consider such issues in their hair-care practices at home than customers who were surveyed before the intervention.

What next?

Since the completion of the project we have applied to the ESRC for funding for knowledge exchange activities to work with our project partners (HABIA, VTCT, City & Guilds) and hairdressing colleges to train the trainers to integrate sustainability issues into the hairdressing curriculum and qualifications, thus increasing impact still further. For example while one hairdresser can influence hundreds of customers, just one trainer can influence hundreds of hairdressers.[2]

References

Ajzen, I. (1985) 'From Intentions to Actions: A Theory of Planned Behavior', in J. Kuhl and J. Beckmann (eds.), *Action Control: From Cognition to Behavior* (New York: Springer-Verlag).

Baden, D. (2010) *An Investigation into the Awareness of Sustainable Development Practices within the Hairdressing Industry* (Southampton, UK: University of Southampton).

Baden, D. (2013) 'What Hairdressers Can Tell Us About Sustainability', https://www.youtube.com/watch?feature=player_embedded&v=0mP0gnSSAhI, accessed 27 June 2014.

Jackson, T. (2005) *Motivating Sustainable Consumption: A Review of Evidence on Consumer Behaviour and Behavioural Change* (Report to the Sustainable Development Research Network; Guildford, UK: University of Surrey).

McKenzie-Mohr, D. (2000) 'Fostering Sustainable Behavior through Community-based Social Marketing', *American Psychologist* 55.5: 531-37.

Oceja, L., and J. Berenguer (2009) 'Putting Text in Context: The Conflict between Pro-Ecological Messages and Anti-Ecological Descriptive Norms', *Spanish Journal of Psychology* 12.2: 657-66.

Williamson, D., G. Lynch-Wood and J. Ramsay (2006) 'Drivers of environmental behaviour in manufacturing SMEs and the implications for CSR', *Journal of Business Ethics* 67.3: 317-30.

Wymenga, P., V. Spanikova, A. Barker, J. Konings and E. Canton (2012) *SMEs in 2012: At the Crossroads. Annual Report on Small and Medium-sized Enterprises in the EU, 2011/12* (Brussels: European Commission).

---

2 More details on our project can be viewed via our 13 minute TEDx talk (Baden 2013).

14 *Embedding a societal view of business among first-year undergraduates*

Colm McLaughlin and Andrea Prothero

UCD School of Business, University College Dublin

Dublin, Republic of Ireland

Introduction

The majority of our students enter the School of Business with the view that business is about profit maximisation and that we will teach them the financial skills to do just that. This view is surprising given the financial and social crisis that Ireland has being going through since 2008; bank bailouts to the tune of €64 billion, 5 years of austerity budgets, a collapse in consumer demand, mass emigration, unemployment peaking at over 14%, and unfinished 'ghost' housing estates across the country as property prices plummeted and developers became insolvent. The relationship between business and society, and the potential for business to impact in a significant and negative way upon society, has been front page news for over 5 years. Perhaps young budding business leaders do not follow the news! They are surprised to find a different perspective on business presented from day one. As part of the UCD School of Business's response to the crisis, the decision was taken to include the relationship between business and society as a fundamental component of our degree programmes. 'Business in Society' now forms one of three core 'pillars' of our undergraduate degree programmes (the others being 'Innovation and Enterprise' and 'Personal Development Planning'). As part of the 'Business in Society' pillar, all 550 incoming students take a 'business in society' module in the first semester of the first year. The message we wish to embed is that this is not an optional extra, but is central to a business education. This essay focuses on this core year one module.

Challenge

This module seeks to challenge the dominant shareholder value perspective held by students coming into the School of Business, to expose them to a range of different perspectives and to encourage students to begin to think critically about the relationship between business and society. This incorporates the UN Principles for Responsible Management Education. We want our students to be the 'future generators of sustainable value for business and society at large', and to be global socially responsible leaders. At the same time, we want to go beyond what is still a managerial view of the firm, as we do not think this perspective is comprehensive enough. A management perspective is one lens we adopt, but we also consider issues from a range of other societal perspectives, including more radical critiques of business and contemporary capitalism.

Bridgman (2011) makes the argument in analysing business ethics case studies that the typical approach focuses on ethical dilemmas that individual managers or individual companies might face in balancing the competing interests of a range of stakeholders. Implicit in this approach is the assumption that irresponsible corporate behaviour can be resolved through more ethical leadership. But as Bridgman (2011: 312) notes, if the widely advocated solution is to teach more business ethics, then the problem as it currently stands must simply be one of the 'moral deficiencies of managers'. This approach ignores social, political and ideological factors. In doing so, it ignores the structural features of deregulated shareholder capitalism. As Thompson (2003, 2013) argues in his 'disconnected capitalism thesis', individual managers and firms may wish to act more responsibly (towards communities, suppliers, their employees and other stakeholders), but they are unable to keep their side of the bargain due to the demands of institutional investors and the fluidity of capital markets. CSR and responsible leadership are therefore not uncontroversial topics and we wish to expose students to debates about how effective a CSR/stakeholder view of the firm might be in resolving some of the pressing environmental and social issues of our times (McLaughlin 2013). We want them to consider deeper questions such as:

- Is CSR a real attempt on the part of companies to grapple with important social, ethical and environmental issues as opposed to window-dressing behaviour to appeal to consumer idealism and pre-empt government regulation?
- What role should the state play in regulating business?
- Do corporations have too much power and influence?
- Are contemporary forms of capitalism and consumption part of the problem when it comes to issues such as climate change?

What we did

Steiner and Steiner's (2011) *Business, Government and Society* textbook provides us with a useful framework to organise such questions. Adapting their framework, we present students with four approaches to business and society: market capitalism, the stakeholder model, regulatory pluralism and critical perspectives. We outline the framework and then utilise it throughout the module to analyse a range of contemporary 'business in society' issues, such as labour standards in supply chains, evasion of corporation tax, the Irish financial crisis, gender inequality at work, sustainability and unethical marketing. Beyond challenging the dominant shareholder view of the firm, we do not push one particular approach; rather we aim to create an environment in which students can explore different perspectives and make informed choices about the role they believe business should play in society. Lively discussions in the lectures (there are four classes of between 100 and 150 students) form an important part of the process, as do the assessment techniques we utilise, and it is these we focus on further here as we believe these may have some wider use for colleagues interested in responsible management pedagogy. Following Bridgman's (2011) call for more cases that integrate the potential for an analysis of economic, political and ideological issues, we have written a number of short cases that highlight a range of perspectives on corporate behaviour. Students are not asked to analyse the case from the perspective of the firm, but from the perspective of an advocate of each of the four models in the framework. By doing so, we do not ask students to justify their own view on the case, which in our experience either tends to be the perspective a student started a module with or else is the perspective they think the lecturer holds and is therefore the perceived 'right' answer. Rather, we invite them to briefly adopt each perspective as a way of exploring with an open mind the arguments that advocates of different positions hold. In doing so, we aim to highlight the complexity of many business in society issues. We feel this approach will lead to students forming a more informed opinion on important issues in their own time, while also sowing the seeds for the remainder of their degree that when it comes to understanding the relationship between business and society there is no 'right' answer.

The second assessment method utilised is a formal team debate that each student participates in once during the semester; the debates take place fortnightly in groups of 20–25 and are led by tutors. Students are assigned to a side of a moot, which often means they will be arguing for a perspective they may not personally agree with. As with our approach to the case study, this opens students up to different arguments in a non-threatening way. The debate allows both the participants and the audience to see that there are often contrasting but legitimate perspectives on an issue. Those students who are not participating in the debate in a given week must also submit a summary sheet outlining their opinions on the key arguments presented. These summary sheets form a small percentage of final marks for the module, and ensure a good turnout and lively discussion following the formal debate. Some of the moots we have used recently include:

- CSR is nothing more than 'greenwash' and corporate PR-spin
- Capitalism is bad for the environment
- The 'business case' approach to addressing gender inequality is ineffective

What happened

We have now been running the module for three years, and while we have updated the content to reflect recent changes and developments in the broad responsible management arena we have stuck with the assessment strategies of a case study and student debates. What both have shown us is that there is significant engagement with the different perspectives in both students' response to the case question and throughout the debates. Students come into the programme with a shareholder value view of the firm but by the end of the semester there is a noticeable shift in their views. They also report enjoying the debate, despite finding it slightly challenging and nerve-wracking. Student evaluations for the module are favourable and when asked what three aspects of the module most helped the students' learning, the debates feature highly (the case study forms part of the final assessment so no comments are available for this in the student evaluations). Written feedback from students included:

> A very interactive module that gets you thinking about contemporary issues of business and society... A thought provoking module.

> Enjoyed the debate assignment as it taught me how to research more in depth and how to construct a good argument.

Huge amount of class interaction, importance placed on having own opinion on different elements.

The debate not only challenged me personally but also helped me to successfully understand the material on a deeper level.

The debates motivated me to do independent research, and helped me with my confidence to stand up and speak to an audience. The linked videos of documentaries and debates gave me a greater understanding of how what I was learning applied to real life scenarios.

A lot of the material was thought provoking and gave you a chance to develop opinions on the issues that were being covered.

What next?

As we move into the fourth year of the programme we will continue to build on this approach for the next academic year, and seek to challenge students' preconceived view of the firm as they enter university for the first time. The main objectives of the module are to embed a societal view of business among students while also using assessment strategies to engender critical thinking and independent learning. These lay the foundation both for the 'Business in Society' pillar and in developing learning strategies, with subsequent modules in the degree programme building on these aims. In order to evaluate how effective the module has been, and the extent to which the module has been built on throughout the degree programme, we intend conducting research among our final year students about the role they think business should play in contemporary society.

References

Bridgman, T. (2011) 'Beyond the Manager's Moral Dilemma: Rethinking the 'Ideal-Type' Business Ethics Case', *Journal of Business Ethics* 94: 311-322.

McLaughlin, C. (2013) 'Corporate Social Responsibility and Human Resource Management', in R. Carberry and C. Cross (eds.), *Human Resource Management: A Concise Introduction* (Basingstoke, UK: Palgrave Macmillan).

Steiner, J., and G. Steiner (2011) *Business, Government, and Society: A Managerial Perspective, Text and Cases* (New York: McGraw-Hill, 13th edn).

Thompson, P. (2003) 'Disconnected Capitalism: Or Why Employers Can't Keep their Side of the Bargain', *Work, Employment and Society* 17.2: 359-78.

Thompson, P. (2013) 'Financialization and the Workplace: Extending and Applying the Disconnected Capitalism Thesis', *Work, Employment and Society* 27.3: 472-88.

15 Integrating ethics into business school teaching: The importance of positive role models

Denise Baden

School of Management, University of Southampton

Southampton, England

Introduction

I am the PRME liaison officer for the School of Management, University of Southampton and we are keen to ensure our students graduate predisposed to be responsible business leaders, able and motivated to contribute positively to society. This case study addresses the themes relating to 'How we engage students' and 'How we design teaching and learning' based on the PRME principles of 'developing the capabilities of students' and 'designing effective learning experiences'.

Challenge

One key challenge faced in teaching business ethics is the prevalent cynicism relating to business. Cynicism is a problem because it can become self-fulfilling. For example my research (Baden 2014) showed a significant positive association between beliefs that businesses are unethical with unethical behavioural intentions. This was mostly mediated by reduced self-efficacy, beliefs that it would be difficult for business to behave ethically and yet still be successful undermined motivation even to try. In addition, it is understandable that one would not want to be disadvantaged by obeying the rules if others were gaining a competitive advantage by routinely breaking them. Importantly this cynicism also seems to be overstated. For example the media and documentaries typically focus on business scandals, giving a misleading impression that all business is typically unethical. The factor that had the most influence on behavioural intentions was self-efficacy, so this indicated that showing students examples of businesses that are ethical and successful is important, as is showing them how business can go about creating more positive impacts and reducing any negative impacts.

What we did

The tone and content of the courses relating to CSR and to business ethics were adapted so as to provide inspiring examples of how businesses can adopt more sustainable and responsible practices. The 'How' question was addressed at the level of both the organisation and of individual employees. Examples of class activities and readings designed to highlight positive examples are as follows:

1. Students are asked to find an exemplary case of ethical business (e.g. via BITC website, Ethisphere, sustainability awards, etc.) and summarise why they think it is a positive case study. In the following class they each summarise to their group why they think this deserves to be voted the most ethical business, paying attention to what management practices are involved. Then the group votes on which is the most ethical business in their group and the winner from each group presents to the class, who then vote, and the winner gets a bar of fair-trade chocolate

2. Students are asked to subscribe to one or more of these e-newsletters. Prior to class they read two or three news

stories and post (on the intranet) a brief summary of what they read.

- http://www.ethicalcorp.com/
- http://www.ethicalperformance.com/pages/emailnews.php
- http://www.sustainability.com/login

3. Students are asked to explore examples of how human resource management (HRM) can contribute positively to an organisation's impacts.

- http://about.bankofamerica.com/en-us/global-impact/employee-programs.html

- http://issuu.com/duon/docs/remuneratierapport#

- http://www.theguardian.com/environment/cif-green/2009/apr/08/emissions-carbon-bonuses

- http://thegoodhuman.com//2010/09/09/companies-that-reward-employees-for-going-green/

- http://www.simply-communicate.com/case-studies/communication/how-nokia-made-environmentalism-relevant-its-employees

- http://www.theguardian.com/environment/2010/may/18/bonuses-carbon-emissions

- http://www.wbcsd.org/Pages/EDocument/EDocumentDetails.aspx?ID=47&NoSearchContextKey=true

While the above are useful for showing how to manage an ethical business at the organisational level, I also include examples of how students can be ethical at the individual level. For the individual this may involve resisting pressure to be unethical, or being an organisational activist to encourage the organisation to raise its standards: for example with respect to supply chain management or environment management. In doing so I can get them to roleplay and discuss issues such as when and how to whistleblow or how to present an argument for alternative courses of action. A useful reading for this is *Giving Voice to Values* by Mary Gentile. An example worksheet is shown below.

A. Sarah has just joined a firm of independent financial consultants and hopes to earn good money. She finds out that the advisers, who are supposed to be independent as they are paid by their client, always steer their clients towards the financial products where they receive the highest commission, rather than the one that is best for their client. This seems to be a clear conflict of interest, but when she queries this practice, the manager says it isn't commission as the consultants don't get paid this directly. However, it's a small company and this practice affects the profits and thus has a big effect on the size of the annual bonus which can be as much as 20% of salary. Imagine you are Sarah. What could/would/should you do?

- What organisational factors might make it easy/difficult for you to behave ethically?
- What individual factors might make it easy/difficult for you to behave ethically?
- Which stakeholders are harmed by the present situation?
- What rights do the stakeholders have and what duties does the firm owe to these stakeholders?
- Assuming that you want to behave ethically, consider how you might go about addressing the situation ethically if you were to find yourself in that scenario. First consider how you would approach this situation as an employee: discuss among yourselves what would be the best and most effective way to voice your concerns and achieve a change to more responsible business practices
- Now assume you are the manager in charge. How might you go about ensuring responsible conduct on the part of the business and your employees?

B. You are the buyer for a large company. The current practice is to negotiate hard to keep costs down with existing suppliers and choose the cheapest when sourcing new suppliers. You are aware that several of the suppliers have poor employee and/or environmental standards and think your company could improve its procurement practices.

I also encourage students to consider how they can be more ethical by setting pre-seen exam questions which force them to think these aspects through, for example:

A leading successful electronics company has been accused of unsustainable working practices. Its carbon footprint is high due to high energy costs and wastage, owing to its own business practices and because of the way in which products are marketed, used and disposed of by customers.

How can this issue be addressed at:

- The individual level e.g. assuming you are a senior manager at this firm
- The organisational level
- Sector level
- Institutional level

Consider what could be done to address this issue at each of these levels. Where do you think the most effective changes can occur? Give real life examples where you can to illustrate your points.

During the course, the students will have been exposed to many useful ideas and examples that relate to this question, for example:

- How to present a case to the board. Gathering of arguments and examples and allies
- Codes of conduct, mission statements, ethical culture, governance, ISO14001, cradle to cradle, industrial ecology, circular economy, sustainable business model, take back scheme, targets, and examples such as Interface
- Sector-wide codes of conduct, partnerships with NGOs such as Greenpeace, WWF, WBSCD initiative
- Carbon trading schemes, regulations, laws, sustainable procurement, CRC

What happened

I have gradually changed my focus from presenting ethics scandals, to presenting case studies of ethical businesses. However I do also consider the constraints on ethical business presented by the external competitive market, which can create pressures for cost cutting that undermine genuine ethical business. I deal with this by showing what is being done, for example to combat sweat-shops, but also asking students to critically assess where potential influence over such issues occurs: at consumer level (e.g. by buying fair-trade, boycotts, etc.), organisational level (by policies) or at the institutional/political level.

The quality of responses to the exam question shown above indicates that students do seem to be more aware not just of ethical problems, but also their solutions. In further classroom research I also found that students exposed to positive role models of business were more highly motivated to behave ethically and had greater self-efficacy; they showed more confidence that they would be able to behave ethically in the business domain than those exposed to negative examples of business such as Enron (Baden, 2012).

References

Baden, D. (2012) 'The Effect of Normative Beliefs on Ethical Intentions: Implications for Pedagogy', paper presented at the *25th EBEN Annual Conference 'Work, Virtues and Flourishing'*, IESE, Barcelona.
Baden, D. (2014) 'Look on the Bright Side: A Comparison of Positive and Negative Role Models in Business Ethics Education', *Academy of Management Learning & Education* 14.

16 *An (un)sustainability lesson*

Jack Christian

Manchester Metropolitan University Business School

Manchester, England

Introduction

It is with trepidation that I submit this lesson to a publication that includes the words *Inspirational Guide* in its title. However it is concerned with what I believe to be the single most important issue of our time—sustainability. My lesson is a simple field trip, a walk around east Manchester. In the course of the walk I endeavour to show students on my postgraduate unit, Accounting for Society and Environment, the effects of industrialisation, and get them to think about whether and how we need to change things in the future. The idea of a walk is hardly eye-catching or original but I believe in the context of sustainability it is a powerful tool. Relatively easy to organise, I use this walk to bring home the way humans impact on the environment. Further, because it is a different experience from the usual business school outings, it is a memorable one for most students.

Aims

Sustainability is notoriously difficult to define; for me it is about the survival of the planet and its environment and, therefore, human life and society. What could be more important than that? Unfortunately it would seem sustainability is under threat. According to the UN Economic and Social Council (2011: 1) there is 'widespread concern that the model of development that is evident across the globe is unsustainable'. Obviously this state of affairs has to change and the UN Council notes that education has an important role to play. In particular the Council suggests a number of competences for educators. My lesson builds on three of these (ibid.: 7) in that it:

- Creates opportunities for sharing ideas and experiences from different disciplines/places/cultures/generations without prejudice and preconceptions
- Critically assesses processes of change in society and envisions sustainable futures
- Facilitates participatory and learner-centred education that develops critical thinking and active citizenship

However, building these competences into an accounting course is not without its problems.

Challenge

Collison *et al.* (2007) note the key role of the profession in accounting education and its influence on higher education institutions keen to obtain exemptions for their students. Pre-2007 the profession appeared to have little interest in sustainability, although it is probably true to say this is now changing. However, as yet this change is still not fully reflected in their examination syllabi. Despite that, in my view at least, as higher education practitioners we cannot wait; we must be at the forefront of professional development, not in the rear; after all 'Education is the most vital of all resources...education, which fails to clarify our central convictions, is mere training or indulgence' (Schumacher, 1973).

Perhaps because of this lack of emphasis in accounting practice there is little help in accounting education literature for the accounting educator trying to 'bring the cold wind of sustainability into the classroom' (Gray, 2011: 14). Certainly I have found it hard to focus student attention on the problems facing us while in a classroom setting; they have heard it all before and at the first mention of sustainability, eco or green they switch over to (to them) other more relevant topics. To combat this I took a lead from the ecopsychology movement; I decided to take my postgraduate students out of the classroom and into the world where they could see unsustainability in action.

The lesson

The walk starts at the business school entrance and quickly joins the Rochdale Canal as it passes under London Road. We then join the Ashton Canal and head out into Ancoats. The canals provide plenty of opportunity to talk about the history of Manchester and the Industrial Revolution. I also ask what role, if any, do the canals have in the future? Discussions range from tourism to transport to water distribution. We leave the canal at Beswick Street and drop down to Ashton New Road and cross over the new tram system. Here there are more opportunities to discuss transport systems as well as carbon emissions and cities in general. Should we be bringing huge numbers of people into cities to work or should work be out there in communities?

We then walk along a path by the River Medlock which passes through a small wood on the way to Ardwick. More discussion on the importance of waterways and rivers in particular and, as the woods are full of birds and plants, the importance of biodiversity and maybe protecting what little nature we have left in cities. I note that we are now in the middle of the huge slum clearances of the 1960s and we discuss the impacts of the diaspora on the local community. We reach Ashton Old Road and see evidence of the old railway systems that covered east Manchester. Most of the tracks are gone but it is obvious how important they were to the building of Manchester by the sheer area of land given over to sidings and the number of lines heading into the city. We pause at Ardwick Station to look across the landscape of the city from the passenger bridge between the platforms and to view the rubbish disposal plant now operating in the former sidings: a reminder of the city's more ugly requirements. From here we have a clear view of the modern city juxtaposed with the dereliction of the past. How, I ask, will the modern city look in 80 years' time?

The return to the business school is via Ardwick Green, a little oasis of flowers and trees in the centre of what was an industrial area. Provided for whose benefit, I ask? The local population or perhaps the mill owners and traders of Manchester who chose to congregate in this, the wealthy neighbourhood of its day?

What happened

There is no doubt that the walk catches students' interest; they share ideas and experiences drawn from their own homes and cultures and they begin to assess how society has changed and is changing. Hopefully this is the start of a more critical evaluation of how society functions and more active citizenship as recommended by the UN Economic and Social Council (2011).

I have led five such walks and highlights have included watching Asian students take photos of the Canada geese on the canal. They cannot believe such creatures live in the city centre. At the other extreme I remember the words of one Asian student who remarked, 'I would never have believed places like this existed in England'. She was genuinely shocked at the dereliction in Ancoats; she had not realised that Western modernity and industrialisation could leave such squalor behind. The students all begin to tell each other about their own homes and cultures and share in the learning process. Minds open to new possibilities. Surely this is what education is about.

With regard to my own unit, this is what the walk is aimed at, opening my students' minds to the impact of the current way of doing business and making it easier for them to understand why we have to assess alternative approaches and even evaluate the role played by accounting. Accounting is not a neutral activity. Generally speaking it supports the status quo and incumbent power structures (Puxty, 1993; Tinker and Gray, 2003; Spence, 2007). As future accountants they need to understand this.

What next?

I would love to make this lesson a part of every undergraduate course at Manchester Metropolitan Business School (MMUBS) and this year I am making a start on that dream. I am leading all our first-year marketing students on the walk, all 250 of them, but obviously in a number of tranches. If we at MMUBS are to teach responsible management as required by our commitment to the PRME initiative, we should not be afraid of exploring the effects of irresponsible management. The walk takes about 90 minutes and fits into most tutorials. I have yet to teach a student who did not enjoy the walk and get benefit from it. It addresses one if not the most important issue of our time and it better prepares our students for citizenship.

References

Collison, D., J. Ferguson. and L. Stevenson (2007) 'Sustainability Accounting and Education', in J. Unerman, J. Bebbington and B. O'Dwyer (eds.), *Sustainability Accounting and Accountability* (London: Routledge).

Gray, R. (2011) 'Sustainability and Accounting Education: The Elephant in the Classroom', unpublished paper prepared for *BAFA SIG on Accounting Education Conference*, Winchester, May 2011.

Puxty, A.G. (1993) *The Social and Organizational Context of Management Accounting* (London: Academic Press).

Schumacher, E.F. (1973) *Small is Beautiful* (London: Abacus).

Spence, C. (2007) 'Social and Environmental Reporting and Hegemonic Discourse', *Accounting, Auditing and Accountability* 20.6: 855-882.

Tinker, T., and R. Gray (2003) 'Beyond a Critique of Pure Reason: From Policy to Praxis in Environmental and Social Research', *Accounting, Auditing and Accountability* 16.5: 727-761.

United Nations Economic and Social Council (2011) 'Learning for the Future: Competences in Education for Sustainable Development', *Minutes of the 6th Meeting of UN Economic Commission for Europe Steering Committee on Education for Sustainable Development*, Geneva, 7–8 April 2011.

17 Creating ethical awareness through interactive group work

Radi Haloub and Eshani Beddewela

University of Huddersfield Business School

Huddersfield, England

Introduction

This case story describes how interactive group work was used as a pedagogical method to develop first-year undergraduate students' awareness and appreciation of corporate responsibility. The University of Huddersfield Business School signed up to PRME in 2012 and steps are being undertaken to integrate Principle 3 into the School's curriculum, mainly via a review of 'responsibility' across the teaching and learning strategy of the School. The case story is related to a first-year undergraduate module titled Contemporary Issues in Business. The cohort of students mostly comprise home (UK) students as well as international students from Asia, Africa and Europe. The module aims, first, to develop an awareness of the ethical and social responsibility issues related to business practices and, second, to enable students to engage critically with these issues and develop viable business solutions to resolve the issues.

Challenge

There were several challenges identified in achieving the two module aims mentioned above. First, it was important to select suitable pedagogical methods which would *engage* the students while encouraging *collective thinking*. Second, students had to be taught ethics and social responsibility, so that they could not only *identify* and *understand* these concepts, but more importantly be able to resolve related issues from a *business perspective*.

The question of pedagogy is pervasive across subjects related to the broader domain of business ethics. Several authors have highlighted the difficulties in resolving the theoretical with the practical (Small and Dickie 2003), as well as the philosophical, principle-based moral reasoning domain of ethics with the strategic domain of business and management (Singer 2013). A range of pedagogical methods were used in this module, from simple case studies exploring different ethical and social responsibility dilemmas, to documentary videos to provide students with a visual representation of socially irresponsible business activities.

There is, at present, increased attention being paid to teaching business ethics in higher education in the UK (Cowton and Cummins 2003). Therefore, in addressing the second challenge, it was important that an *objective* point of view was maintained. Students were required to critically analyse the cases and provide viable solutions to the identified ethical and social responsibility dilemmas, and then justify their solutions taking into consideration the resultant consequences for society, business and global markets.

What we did

In order to address the above mentioned challenges, several actions were taken. First, real-life cases, highlighting ethical and/ or social responsibility dilemmas, widely publicised in the news media and which were deemed to explore practical business challenges, were selected for group discussion and debate. The main objective here was to provide the students with a pervasive *appreciation* of social responsibility and ethics. In practice, once students were handed the case, they were asked to first (within 10 to 15 minutes) generate individual solutions for the business dilemma that the ethical and/or social responsibility issue raised. Then the students were asked to work in groups and discuss their individual solutions with the other group members. This was considered to be an effective method, as each student was motivated to justify his or her own individual solution and/or perspective of the ethical dilemma. Given that the student cohort was culturally diverse, the above method resulted in a robust discussion of the dilemma.

The bipolar components of ethical analysis proposed by Singer (2013) were used to guide the group discussions. For example, the students were asked to utilise bipolar components such as value priorities (efficiency vs. justice), strategic responses to market limitations (exploit vs. compensate), stakeholder vs. shareholder-oriented business systems (Freeman's vs. Friedman's theories) and timing (change over time, between now and the future). The groups were then asked to present their *collective* solutions or perspectives to the class.

One of examples used in the seminars related to the use of child labour in the supply chain of a leading UK clothing retailer. Value priorities of the company were used as the bipolar component in the ethical analysis of this particular case. The discussion focused on how the values of 'efficiency' (i.e. cost minimisation and economies of scale) could result in the sacrificing of 'justice' values. Students also argued that the 'perception' of child labour is different across countries and it could be perceived in a more positive manner in some developing countries as the company is providing a livelihood for the children and their families.

The approach discussed above (using similar examples) not only encouraged student participation in the module seminars, but also encouraged them, via the interactive pedagogy, to engage in a high level of critical thinking. While an exposition of ethical/ social responsibility theory may provide students with an appreciation of the subject matter, if as future business leaders students' *actions* and *perceptions* related to social responsibility are to be influenced, then it is important that students *think critically about the consequences* of business activities.

What happened

Student feedback (53 out of 70 students) was obtained after a 12 week teaching period. Students were asked to state their level of agreement with the following points:

1. The module helped me in realising the importance of ethics and corporate responsibility in my personal decision-making as a student and as a future business leader
2. The materials, processes and environment supported effective learning experiences for responsible leadership
3. The module encouraged me as a student to debate current issues related to global corporate responsibility

The percentages of students who strongly agreed and agreed with the previously mentioned three points were calculated as follows: 74%, 83%, and 77%, respectively. There was also a general consensus among the students that they would like to engage more with guest speakers from industry, who manage social responsibility and sustainability in businesses, so that a more practical experience can be obtained.

What next?

The same cohort of students at present have been tasked with developing viable strategies (in groups) to overcome identified business dilemmas, related to ethical and social responsibility issues across a range of business activities. This is integrated into the assessment of this module in the form of a group presentation. Looking forward, the expectation is to revise and reshape this module, keeping the above-mentioned *discussion and debate* method for seminars, but integrating more practice-based teaching via guest speaker sessions for the lectures.

References

Cowton, C., and J. Cummins (2003) 'Teaching Business Ethics in UK Higher Education: Progress and Prospects', *Teaching Business Ethics* 7.1: 37-54.

Singer, A. (2013) 'Teaching Ethics Cases: A Pragmatic Approach', *Business Ethics: A European Review* 22.1: 16-31.

Small, M.W., and L. Dickie (2003) 'Conjoining Ethical Theory and Practice: An Australian Study of Business, Accounting, and Police Service Organizations', *Teaching Business Ethics* 7.4: 379-393.

18 *The development of the Henley Business School MA in Leadership programme*

Jean-Anne Stewart, Stephen Simister and Lynn Thurloway

Henley Business School, University of Reading

Reading, England

Introduction

> Henley Business School was established in 1945, one of the oldest business schools in Europe and one of the top 1% holding triple accreditation. We aim to empower individuals to become great professionals and outstanding business leaders who think with clarity and act with confidence.

This case study presents an overview of a three year project to design and develop a Master's in Leadership programme at Henley Business School within the School of Leadership, Organisations and Behaviour (LOB). As a leading international provider of management education, developing strategies that underpin and sustain a culture of responsible management education, particularly in leadership is core to activities within the Business School and LOB.

Challenge

The leadership development industry has grown exponentially over the past 30 years, with about US$14 billion spent annually in the US alone on leadership development (Gurdjian *et al.*, 2014).

Ironically, during this same period, there have been more and more cases of 'poor leadership'. A recent UK study (Gitsham 2009) reported that only 7% of managers stated that their companies effectively develop global business leaders.

Against this background, this research project was designed to inform curriculum design and pedagogy (or 'andragogy'; Knowles, 1984) of master's-level programmes in a triple-accredited international business school, to develop 'better' or more effective leaders. Leadership today is complex, challenging and demanding, with leaders facing 'wicked problems' (Grint, 2008). It is not surprising that short 'Executive Education' style programmes seem to have no significant impact on leaders facing such challenges. This project aimed to design a programme that would effect a real behavioural change in practising leaders through a new postgraduate, post-experience MA Leadership programme.

What we did

The programme design team, a small group of faculty at Henley Business School, agreed the following key design principles to underpin the development of the new Master's in Leadership programme. The programme:

- Is relevant and authentic to both leaders and organisational practice
- Recognises that leadership and leadership development is experiential, iterative, explorative and behaviourally based
- Develops leaders that are resilient and flexible
- Supports a culture of continuous learning, reflection and personal change
- Is driven by the challenges and demands from contemporary leadership practice with theoretical dimensions supporting, informing, engaging and developing knowledge, understanding, learning and debate

- Is flexible and adaptable in terms of different contexts—including sectors, size of organisation and international base

What happened

To address these principles and recognising the ongoing debate around rigour and relevance of business school programmes, the design team invited organisational practitioners to form an **advisory group** to debate challenges for today's leaders and contribute to the design and development of the programme, so that real world issues enhance and inform more traditional, theory-driven approaches. This group comprised an eclectic mix of people representing a wide range of organisations including: large global corporates, government departments, academic institutions, small enterprises, voluntary sector and business advisers. All had a common desire and interest in leadership and contributed openly. The programme development was organised through one-day workshops, scheduled over two years, where crucial elements were presented and critiqued within a dialectic environment. This resulted in consensus on a **programme** designed to offer:

- Flexible and part-time courses to fit in with challenging full-time leadership roles
- Summer schools and intensive workshops which maximise immersive learning opportunities but minimise time away from day-to-day commitments
- Assignments and projects which produce practical benefits and key recommendations to the participants' organisations within a few weeks of the start of the programme
- Personal leadership development for the participant which will provide an immediate impact on the participants' teams and other stakeholders in the leaders' organisations
- Opportunity for cross-organisational learning

- Opportunities to experience, 'test' and enhance their leadership by working in areas outside their normal organisational experience through leadership projects in organisations including the third sector and voluntary groups
- Learning as 'doing' to develop behavioural and academic learning through problem-solving and action learning processes
- Assessments to meet external accreditations: for example, AACSB, AMBA, EQUIS, PRME
- Blended learning, using technology to support curriculum content between face-to-face workshops, virtual study teams and virtual action learning
- Applied research projects using a broad range of research methods including combined and mixed methods

The programme has now been fully approved by the University Board of Teaching and Learning and the first intake is planned to start the programme in June 2015, with a one week summer school.

What next?

During the project, several important lessons were learned. First, the high-quality discussions with and contributions of the advisory group really helped inform the programme design to be fully up-to-date and aware of the current challenges of leaders in today's organisations, especially the importance of 'responsible, purposeful leadership'.

The advisory group emphasised that leaders want to learn but also need support to apply what they learn. They commented that: '…hearing about the latest leadership techniques is interesting but to make it relevant, you need to understand how to take it back to your own organisation and apply it'.

During the design process, it also became apparent that we needed to draw on other skills outside the immediate Leadership faculty team within LOB. Being able to draw on colleagues' expertise in the school of Marketing and Relationships enabled the 'responsibility' aspect of Leadership to be more holistically defined and brought into the programme.

The part-time mode of this programme meant that programme members needed support between workshops, particularly with their real leadership challenges and projects, and this is achieved through the use of a blended approach of action learning and virtual action learning. Action learning is not new (Pedler, 2008); it was developed in the 1930s at the University of Cambridge (Revans 1998), where scientists met in groups to discuss their current challenges and ask each other questions, to try to resolve problems for which there is no 'right answer'. Action learning is seen as one of the most effective ways to engage and develop leaders (Stewart 2009) in real, work-based leadership projects, both in day-to-day practice and for project assignments.

It was also apparent from the discussions that traditional approaches that culminate in a dissertation which is driven by theory would not allow participants to develop and apply their learning in the experiential manner which was highlighted as a key principle by the Leadership Advisory Group. Hence, the approach to assessment and especially for the final project was designed to offer participants the opportunity to use real leadership challenges as the central driver for their research and analysis, rather than the traditional academic approach which uses relevant theory as the central driver, for their investigations and assessments. Taking such an approach allows participants to draw on relevant academic principles related to leadership, to develop in order to inform rather than drive their assessment. It also allows them to focus on the applicability of their learning to their own experiences and challenges through synthesis, reflection and evaluation of both practice and theory leading to informed decisions and recommendations. A practice-based approach allows participants to consider the issue that they are investigating in an integrated manner recognising the importance of context, stakeholders and, indeed, their own impact on potential challenges and solutions which the Leadership Advisory Group suggested was a key principle for developing leaders.

References

Gitsham, M. (2009) *Developing the Global Leader of Tomorrow* (Berkhamsted, UK: Ashridge).

Grint, K. (2008) *Leadership, Management and Command: Rethinking D-day* (Basingstoke, UK: Palgrave).

Gurdjian, P., T. Halbeisen and K. Lane (2014) 'Why Leadership-Development Programs Fail', *McKinsey Quarterly*

Knowles, M. (1984) *The Adult Learner: A Neglected Species* (Houston, TX: Gulf Publishing).

Pedler, M. (2008) *Action Learning for Managers* (London: Gower, 2nd edn).

Revans, R. (1998) *ABC of Action Learning* (London: Lemos and Crane).

Stewart, J-A. (2009) 'Evaluation of an Action Learning Programme for Leadership Development', *Action Learning Journal* 6.2 (July 2009).

19 The fusion of a live case company approach with a social dimension: Preparing students for 21st-century business in society

Julie C. Thomson and Anne M.J. Smith

Glasgow Caledonian University

Glasgow, Scotland

Introduction

Glasgow Caledonian University (GCU) is a signatory to the United Nations' Principles for Responsible Management Education (PRME). GCU's participation in PRME is led by the Glasgow School *for* Business and Society (GSBS), an inter-disciplinary school that is home to expertise in business, management, law and social sciences. PRME's focus on social responsibility, ethics and sustainability fits perfectly with the University's values and motto of working for 'The Common Weal' (common good) and is reflected in our choice of Nobel Prize winner, Professor Muhammad Yunus, as Chancellor in 2013. By embracing the PRME agenda, the University is making a conscious effort to provide an education designed to produce responsible, inspiring managers and leaders of the future who can cope with the complex challenges in our globalising world.[1]

---

[1] For more details of the University's commitment to PRME please see www.gcu.ac.uk/prme.

Challenge

The challenge presented here arose during the recent process of reviewing and revising all undergraduate and postgraduate programmes within GSBS to reflect the PRME values of developing leaders for the future we want. As part of this process, programme and module leaders were challenged to redesign modules in a way that clearly incorporated one or more of the PRME principles. This process led to a search for a set of innovative learning activities, environments and assessments, which could challenge and engage students to explore the interface between social values and business challenges. The challenge therefore lay in designing a PRME-centric learning experience for students. This case explains how a project was designed for a third-year undergraduate module called 'Entrepreneurship in Developing Organisations'.

Our starting point is that learning on the module should be significant, meaningful, purposeful and experiential (Knowles *et al.* 2012). We work on the premise that as educators we must create the right conditions to facilitate a learning process that meets the learner's needs, thereby supporting students to achieve self-actualisation, fulfil their potential for personal growth, and empower them to take responsibility for their own learning. This project makes use of a type of learning where the students are required to use skills of self-reflection and critical thinking, which are essential in the contemporary business world.

What we did

Instead of employing 'traditional' teaching methods, the module team adopted 50+20's notion of educators as 'the guide on the side', as opposed to 'sage on the stage'.[2] This led to the development

2   50+20 Management Education for the World, http://50plus20.org, accessed 3 June 2014.

of an interactive project with industry involvement. By using a live case company, we aimed for a student-centred approach that encourages active learning. The project was designed to enable students not only to learn *about* social entrepreneurship but also to *be* socially entrepreneurial. The learning and assessment strategy incorporated a range of approaches which included problem-based learning, cooperative learning, group-learning, enquiry-based learning and technology-enhanced learning (Michael 2006). This will become apparent during the description of the project, which ran as follows:

The **director of the company** presented the company background as well as an insight into the current challenges facing the business. The upbeat, down-to-earth manner of the director meant the students were able to identify well with him, and connect. Consistent with the business world, students were given an opportunity to probe and ask questions (which not all students took up). The students were then set the task of researching entrepreneurial opportunities and to act in a **consultative role**, producing a set of recommendations at the end. Effectively working for a live company motivated the students to engage with the business challenges posed, and they were challenged to develop their problem-solving skills and find a solution.

The project required the students to **work in groups** and use **modern technology**, in the form of a Wiki (a web application which allows people to add, modify or delete content in collaboration with others), as a major means of communication. This technology facilitated the students' interaction with the material and with their peers, and required the practice of skills of information retrieval, selection, analysis and synthesis (Duncan *et al.* 2007). The students contacted community groups, government bodies and other organisations to develop new insights, extend their networks and gain material for their project.

A key feature of the case company was that it held charitable status but also traded through competitive tenders, through which it secured contracts to provide services throughout the UK. Working with a **social entrepreneur** exposed the students to an organisation with a social (as opposed to purely business-driven) mission. Specifically, the aim of the business is to help transform the lives of people affected by drug and alcohol problems. This non-conventional context exposed students to some distressing facts, but also inspiring stories, during their search for material. The context as such helped to engage the students in a project that combined the need to be socially responsible and commercially astute at the same time.

What happened

Students were issued with the project briefs, met with the director, were made aware of confidentiality and ethical responsibilities, and then progressed to search the internet for data that would help them to generate possible business opportunities. Students immediately encountered a vast array of problems: ones of too much information, geographical diversity, confidentiality, ethical decisions, equality issues, and appropriate dialogue with private and public sector organisations around sensitive issues such as alcohol misuse.

Students became more aware of the requirement to prepare themselves in a professional manner which would give them credibility and demonstrate an ability to adopt an ethical approach. Student groups found interesting solutions to complex problems by looking outside the United Kingdom, to Australia and Scandinavia, for exciting opportunities that could be applied in the UK. By learning through practice, and with guidance on how best to construct emails and handle dialogue with external stakeholders, the students discovered methods for handling sensitive subjects in an ethical fashion. The same students in the course of their projects experienced rejection, developed an understanding of how to proceed with less attractive options, and explored ways of turning negative situations into positives and meaningful outcomes.

A dynamic learning environment such as this one, which is both purposeful and student centred, encourages those involved to face situations and tackle issues they may never have encountered, or to explore ways of tackling issues that have affected them directly. The project design created a learning environment that fostered dialogue, partnership working and created knowledge about being socially entrepreneurial through creative thinking, underpinned by facts and hard work.

What next?

The module review to create alignment with PRME resulted in a redesign of a practice-based project in a social business context. Fundamentally, the project design required a fusion of academic concepts within a practice-based learning environment. In the short term, fusing entrepreneurship with social responsibility and ethical business with social enterprise requires further scholarly development to create an applied framework for teaching and learning. In the medium term there is scope to develop the model for implementation across an institution and multiple disciplines. A project of this nature is enabling for a whole range of students, from a classics scholar to a medical student, to understand how being socially entrepreneurial is a fusion of concepts in academic terms and in practice a way of working and living in 21st-century business and society.

References

Duncan, M.J., M. Lyons and Y. Al-Nakeeb (2007) 'You Have to Do It Rather than Being in a Class and Just Listening': The Impact of Problem-based Learning on the Student Experience in Sports and Exercise Biomechanics', *Journal of Hospitality, Leisure, Sport and Tourism Education* 6.1: 71-80.

Knowles, M.S., E.F. Holton and R.A. Swanson (2012) *The Adult Learner: The Definitive Classic in Adult Education and Human Resource Development* (Burlington, MA: Elsevier, 6th edn).

Michael, J. (2006) 'Where's the Evidence that Active Learning Works?' *Advances in Physiology Education* 30.4: 159-167.

20 *Communicating sustainability in 59 seconds*

John Blewitt

Aston Business School

Aston University, Birmingham, England

Introduction

Aston Business School (ABS) has gained a deserved reputation for providing its students with very valuable knowledge, skills and understanding, enabling them to successfully operate and sometimes achieve great things in an increasingly competitive and harsh economic environment. The School works with business, public sector bodies and third sector organisations, recognising that its location in Birmingham, Europe's most culturally diverse city, allows its work locally to have global resonance. A key aspect of this resonance is a growing commitment to ethical and sustainably literate research-led teaching and learning experience. This commitment pre-dates PRME but has been significantly reinforced by it.

ABS' undergraduate and postgraduate degree programmes aim to nurture students' capabilities and capacities to become responsible business leaders and global citizens.[1]

---

[1] Details of the School's commitment to social responsibility and sustainability can be found at: http://www1.aston.ac.uk/ aston-business-school/about-abs/srs/

Challenge

In 2011 ABS launched a new postgraduate taught Master's programme, the MSc Social Responsibility and Sustainability. In its first
year it was offered as a full- and part-time course for on-campus
students, and in 2012 a wholly online version was launched. Both
versions aim to attract young and mid-career professionals in any
field looking to enhance their knowledge and commitment to creating new ways of doing business. Although designing and delivering the programme for online delivery had its own challenges,
particularly for those faculty members wary of the vagaries as well
as affordances of digital media technology, both versions run successfully in parallel and sometimes in a more integrated fashion.
Online students frequently share ideas, values, concerns, experiences and hopes with those on campus in the hybrid digital space
created by Aston's virtual learning environment.

The new programme conjured up other challenges too. One of
these relates to an area often covered in a rather formulaic manner within Business Schools, namely, communication. Communication is an important topic within marketing, advertising and
human resource management, but for a programme that has as its
raison d'être social responsibility and sustainability, communications offers other interesting opportunities. Many of the issues and
problems businesses face are paradoxically and simultaneously
both simple and complex. Understanding sustainability—an *end
in view* stating we must respect the finite ecological limitations of
our planet—and sustainable development—essentially, a *process*
articulating notions of development and sustainability—requires
the student-practitioner to perceive the world *holistically*.

It has become commonplace for sustainability scholars to say
that all things are, in some way, connected. It is also quite reason-
able to suggest that sustainability and sustainable development
are ethical, as well as scientific concepts, although recently we
have witnessed the birth of the new sub-discipline, sustainability
science. This means that the ethical and sustainability challenges

of the 21st century compel us to develop a mindset, a range of capabilities, capacities for disciplinary synthesis, an emotional intelligence and an ability to communicate effectively across disciplines, professions, cultures, social habits and organisational routines. The world of business is a complex and a complicated place, and to cut through the noise, confusion and prejudices enshrined in 'business as usual' cries out for new ethical and sustainability orientated messages to be communicated clearly and distinctly to many different but interconnected publics and interest groups.

The challenge, then, in one of the MSc's modules is to communicate sustainability in 59 seconds.

What we did

This '59 seconds' has quickly become one of the most challenging, enjoyable, creative and dynamic assignments in the whole of the course. In the module 'Communicating Sustainability' students are required to produce a video which will communicate a complex ethical and sustainability message in a simple, vibrant and memorable manner, using sound, still and/or moving images with a minimum use of either spoken or written text. Students undertake a considerable amount of exploratory work on the effectiveness of images in communication campaigns, the psychological effects of colour and tone, the emotional importance of sound, especially music, and the ways in which editing pace and rhythm contributes to the creation of knowledge and understanding non-discursively, sensuously, viscerally, affectively. As human beings, our emotions are an important element in what we know and what we feel, and although this is not to gainsay the importance of reason, logic and the word, it is to say that communication is far more than a written report, essay or figures on a spreadsheet.

A subsidiary objective of this assignment is for the creator to produce a video that both 'works', and has the potential to go 'viral'. Indeed, there are plenty of funny, absurd, serious, clever and stupid video communications that have gone viral or, in the words of Malcolm Gladwell, have spread 'the idea virus'. In the short history of digital social networks, businesses, NGOs, universities, community groups and countless individuals have become enthusiastic content producers for YouTube. However, only a few of these go viral. When they do, the world can, and sometimes does, change.

What happened

The MSc students, both on campus and online, have not usually studied communication, the creative arts, film or media previously. Most are business graduates and many find the most demanding aspect of this assignment to be the unleashing of their latent creativity, which has often been a sacrificial victim of their earlier formal education or their continuing professional development. As one student noted in her evaluation:

> I was truly surprised to discover how good was the work made by the other students and how original it was. It appears that this exercise allowed students to express their point of view, as well as their creativity on a subject, possibility, which is often forgotten in Business studies (in 6 years of studies, it was the first time I was asked to make a presentation that was not a PowerPoint or equivalent).

Consequently, the viral assignment is far more than a business exercise such as an 'elevator pitch', which is often little more than a breathless advertisement for a project or for oneself. The 'viral' draws on all the domains that constitute effective learning, requires deep questioning and reflexivity and, in most cases, requires the acquisition of skills that initially seem alien to a practitioner or student of business. However, students quickly take to Windows Moviemaker or iMovie or Audacity, and their familiarity with smart phone technology gives them an instinctive feel for digital image-based and compressed communication. They also learn from each other, help each other at a distance or in close proximity on campus and sometimes both at the same time. Some actually invest their energies in learning quite sophisticated animation, image-based, audio and editing software downloaded at no cost from the digital cultural commons.

Students will present their initial ideas individually to the group. Then, at a later date, 'screen' and discuss their 'rough cuts'. Other members of the group offer informal, often highly perceptive and sensitive, feedback to the producer. The 'rough cuts' are uploaded on to the MSc's virtual learning environment and the informal peer assessment continues. Preview screenings extend through cyber-time and cyberspace involving everyone. In addition to this, the student, now referred to as 'a creative' as well as a committed sustainability practitioner and business change agent, is invited to reflect on her personal, practical, political and cultural learning experiences in a short piece of writing or audio commentary. This reflection is invariably as creative, affective and as powerful as the audio-visual content itself for students to explore inner motivations, beliefs and values, public issues, technical and aesthetic matters and, quite frequently, the nature of lived experience itself.

What next?

The 'creative', once satisfied with her viral, will submit the '59 seconds' for formal assessment and grading but, more importantly perhaps, she is also invited to screen the movie within Aston to staff or students during the annual Green Week festival of events. This is both a recognition of their success and the first real-world test for their viral, although some may have trialled a rough cut on YouTube beforehand.

Of course, the students want good grades and most of them deservedly get one. However, it is the nature of their learning experience that is fundamental. This has encompassed critical and practical engagement with multi modal analysis and creative production, the reflection on self and the self's place in the wider world, understanding that communicating sustainability requires an acknowledgement of ecological gloom and a need to inspire optimism and positive action in others. The creative viral assignment also frequently gives voice to others, animate or inanimate, sentient or insentient, that are in other business contexts designated as basically forms of capital to be used up in the relentless treadmill of production and consumption.

Recent viral topics have included: animal welfare, climate change, life itself, the five 'Rs', water, social enterprise, the fur trade, oil extraction in the Niger Delta, over fishing, waste, food inequality, the Anthropocene, love, protecting the Antarctic from development, responsible advertising, using ceramic coffee mugs, and much more. Constructing new sustainable ways of doing business requires creativity and innovation and business schools really need to offer learning environments where this flourishes.

As one student noted in his reflective commentary:

> Never was a time I felt that I was taught something in this lecture. Instead I was always given enough time and input to think and reflect critically on the various topics and therefore derive from my very own learning, as well as from other fellow students. I decided to use the same style of conveying the message without explicitly conveying it.

ESD enterprise: 'To a better world', or just 'to the record'?

John Hirst

Durham University Business School

Durham, England

Introduction

This story of Durham University Business School's MBA International Enterprise Project began as a humanitarian response to the Sri Lankan tsunami in 2004. Strong links between various university departments and Sri Lanka led to establishing Project Sri Lanka, providing opportunities for staff and student volunteers to make a contribution to post-tsunami restoration and reconstruction projects.

Challenge

MBA students were invited to provide consultancy expertise for some of these projects, which then led to business projects being initiated by students themselves, and finally to the birth of an accredited MBA module relating to the UN Decade of Education for Sustainable Development (ESD).

The module design sought to avoid inhibiting students' creativity or initiative-taking. Unlike most other MBA modules, it is about problem-based learning (PBL), so students initiate and take ownership of, and are responsible for developing, their own projects. So, what of the teacher's role?

> You are not the oil, you are not the air—merely the point of combustion, the flash-point where the light is born... you are merely the lens in the beam...self-effaced so that it may be focussed or spread wider...to vanish as an end and remain purely a means...[otherwise], you rob the lens of its transparency (Hammarskjold 1997: 96).

What we did

Participants initially had free rein to initiate their own projects including cinnamon production, eco-tourism, sustainable construction, coconut processing, fishing, and elephant sanctuaries, but the university's insurers drew the line at leopard safari camps! In 2012, two INSEAD case studies were introduced into the module, prompting students to initiate larger corporate projects based in the capital city, Colombo, including one with a company operating eco-factories supplying M&S, and another with a company operating eco-hotels. The students are put in touch with these companies but are then responsible for working with them to develop viable projects of mutual interest which they can undertake on a 7-day field-trip, normally involving action-research and even more action-learning.

The structure of the module is based on Mintzberg and Gosling's (2003) 'five manager mindsets': reflective (the way people think); worldly (the international context); analytical (management strategy and organisational dynamics); collaborative (partnerships and relationships); and action (change). We added a sixth mind-set: sustainability (sustainable futures). For pre-course reading we recommend Visser's (2010) *The Quest for Sustainable Business* which *Ethical Performance* cites as 'the most important and, in certain respects, the only historical account of corporate responsibility to date, and a bloody good read'!

The central theme throughout the course is 'Design Thinking' (Martin 2009), affording alternative perspectives on management education and practice, while also serving two important purposes: first to open up debate about intuitive thinking and the integrative values and cognitions required for sustainability literacy and 'obliquity' (Kay 2011); and second, to introduce students to the concept of 'abductive logic' which is not only essential for innovation and creativity, but also for envisaging sustainable futures. The pluralistic context of Sri Lanka, steeped in Buddhism, also lends itself to the application of Schumacher's (1993) 'Buddhist Economics', in other words 'economics for sustainability'.

Learning outcomes are aligned with HEA/QAA ESD guidance on 'Attributes':

- An ability to engage in independent, evidence-based, integrated thinking (integrative cognitions)
- An understanding of values and how they influence perception (integrative values)
- A knowledge of approaches to economic development in an international context (worldly mind-set)
- An ability to reflect on values, beliefs and norms, how they affect decisions and behaviours (reflective mind-set)
- An ability to evaluate actions/impacts and use this information strategically (analytical mind-set)
- An understanding of social and environmental responsibility and the need for transformational learning (sustainability mind-set)
- An ability to take a proactive approach to change and act, even in the face of complexity, ambiguity and uncertainty (action mind-set)
- An ability to engage and collaborate with, and influence, others effectively (collaborative mind-set)
- The capacity to be flexible and adopt a problem-solving mind-set (problem-based learning)
- The vision, motivation and resourcefulness to innovate for sustainable futures (design-thinking)

The module embraces all teaching and learning approaches highlighted in the ESD Guidance, including:

- **Case studies.** Particularly the INSEAD case studies on our host companies, supplied by ECCH
- **Stimulus activities.** Including the 'All Adrift' consensus building exercise, stories (mainly from Anthony De Mello), poetry (particularly Wendy Cope), various videos (including 'Life In A Day' and RSAnimate)
- **Simulation.** Including a collaborative group exercise on managing change and uncertainty based on the 'Parable of the Sadhu' by Buzz McCoy (HBR) which participants map onto a Ketso project mat
- **Experiential project-work.** Action research/learning undertaken as a mini business project in an international setting unfamiliar to the majority of participants, requiring them to step beyond their comfort zones, which they then write up as a collaborative team-work report for their assessment
- **Place-based learning.** Working with organisations that have sustainability truly embedded in their strategies and operations, students particularly learn from their models of stakeholder engagement, supply-chain management, impact assessment, sustainability literacy and reporting, and sustainability marketing

The desired outcome is what Mintzberg (2004) calls 'experienced reflection' fermenting into 'transformational learning', something that occurs 'at the interface where reflective thinking meets practical doing' in 'that space, suspended between experience and explanation, where the mind makes the connections'. This is synonymous with MacIntyre's (2007) 'goods internal to practices', the 'goods' in this case being 'students' attributes, dispositions and competencies rather than just a content-based approach around "what has been learned about sustainability"' (Sterling 2012). 'It means looking in so that you can better see out in order to perceive a familiar thing in a different way' (Mintzberg and Gosling 2003: 4).

To consolidate and capture this effectively, we include a session on reflective practice, in which we encourage students to engage in deep reflective writing (and produce an individual reflective paper as part of their assessment)—this goes way beyond descriptive writing to include 'emotional disclosure' (Pennebaker 1997) which, although initially challenging, is proven to enhance intellectual performance and personal well-being. 'People feel that they have hardly any time for reflection, and since reflective consciousness is one defining characteristic of human nature, the results are profoundly dehumanizing' (Capra 2003: 110).

What next?

While we hope to inculcate a habit of systematic reflection, there is now an even greater imperative. This calls for reflective practice to rescue the values-based right brain hemisphere from relentless onslaught by the utility-obsessed left brain hemisphere, which McGilchrist (2009) believes to be the root cause of unsustainable behaviour resulting in environmental and cultural destruction.

We recommend further research into this potentially profound link between McGilchrist's 'divided brain theory' and ESD. Also, in response to the evident need for a distinctive 'biopsychosocial systems' framework to defend ESD against neutralisation and co-option by the mainstream (Sterling 2012), thereby rendering it 'virtually useless' (Fleming and Jones 2013), we recommend revisiting Spiral Dynamics which Haigh (2011: 10) describes as 'one of the most sophisticated, comprehensive and influential theories of transformative education' that 'offers a unifying framework that makes genuinely holistic thinking and actions possible' (Beck and Cowan 1996: 30).

What the ESD Guidance fails to state clearly enough, unlike Orr (1994), is that

> the crisis we face is first and foremost one of mind, percep-
> tion, and values; hence it is a challenge to those institutions
> presuming to shape minds, perceptions and values. It is an
> educational challenge. More of the same kind of education
> can only make things worse (in Marshall *et al.* 2011).

It could also be clearer about what is really required: a 'courageous and humble' (Eichler 1999) confrontation with the principles on which the currently unsustainable paradigm is founded, grappling with related paradoxes and 'troublesome knowledge' (Meyer and Land 2003), through an 'unflinching critical epistemology' (Fleming and Jones 2013) that dares to be different, risks professional and academic marginalisation, but ultimately prepares students to cross the conceptual 'threshold' to an alternative 'ecologically integrated paradigm' (Boehnert 2012).

One leading city CEO and venture capitalist who took the module related his experience as follows:

> My expectation going into this programme was to make an
> impact in ways that I could relate to. I was intent on exiting
> from the same door I came in with my alpha male status
> intact. I had it all planned; I would leverage all my experi-
> ence and networks that would reflect on my success and
> enable me to create a sense of achievement...for me. And
> then...it then dawned on me that this was not about me
> helping them—whoever they were—but on me reflecting on
> the way other people live their lives and to use this oppor-
> tunity to put aside everything that I stood for. To learn, I had
> first to unlearn and then to trust in the ability of people I did
> not really know. John planted the seed in my mind that we
> should dare to be different. I came out of [this module] by
> way of a very different, more enriching, door.

To quote Kurt Vonnegut

> 'To a better world,' he [Paul] started to say, but he cut the
> toast short, thinking of the people of the Ilium, already
> eager to recreate the same old nightmare. He shrugged. 'To
> the record,' he said, and smashed the empty bottle on a
> rock. Von Neumann considered Paul and then the broken
> glass. 'This isn't the end you know,' he said. 'Nothing ever
> is, nothing ever will be—not even Judgement Day.' 'Hands
> up,' said Lasher, almost gaily. 'Forward March!' (Vonnegut
> 1992: 137)

References

Beck, D., and C. Cowan (1996) *Spiral Dynamics: Mastering Values, Leadership & Change* (Oxford, UK: Blackwell).

Boehnert, J. (2012) 'Epistemological Error: A Whole Systems View of Converging Crises', EcoLabs, http://eco-labs.org/index.php/papers/cat_view/41-papers-to-download-pdfs, accessed 2 July 2014.

Capra, F. (2003) *The Hidden Connections* (London: Flamingo).

Eichler, M. (1999) 'Sustainability from a Feminist Sociological Perspective: A Framework for Disciplinary Reorientation', in E. Becker and T. Jahn (eds.), *Social Sciences & Sustainability: A Cross-disciplinary Approach* (London: Zed): 182-206.

Fleming, P., and M. Jones (2013) *The End of Corporate Social Responsibility: Crisis & Critique* (London: Sage).

Haigh, M. (2011) 'Transformative Learning for Global Citizenship: Turning to Turquoise', *Learning and Teaching in Higher Education* 5 (2010–11): 7-15.

Hammarskjold, D. (1997) *Markings* (London: Faber & Faber, library edition).

Kay, J. (2011) *Obliquity: Why our Goals are Best Achieved Indirectly* (London: Profile).

McGilchrist, I. (2009) *The Master & His Emissary: The Divided Brain and the Making of the Western World* (New Haven, CT: Yale University Press).

MacIntyre, A. (2007) *After Virtue: A Study in Moral Theory* (Notre Dame, IN: University of Notre Dame Press, 3rd edn).

Marshall, J., G. Coleman and P. Reason (2011) *Leadership for Sustainability* (Sheffield, UK: Greenleaf Publishing).

Martin, R. (2009) *The Design of Business: Why Design Thinking is the Next Competitive Advantage* (Boston, MA: Harvard Business Press).

Meyer, J., and R. Land (2003) *Threshold Concepts and Troublesome Knowledge: Linkages to Ways of Thinking and Practising within the Disciplines* (ETL Occasional Report 4; Edinburgh: University of Edinburgh).

Mintzberg, H. (2004) *Managers Not MBAs* (London: FT-Prentice Hall).

Mintzberg, H., and J. Gosling (2003) 'The Five Minds of a Manager', *Harvard Business Review*, November 2003: 1-9.

Pennebaker, J. (1997) 'Writing About Emotional Experiences as a Therapeutic Process', *Psychological Science* 8.3 (May 1997): 162-166.

Schumacher, E. (1993) *Small is Beautiful: A Study of Economics as if People Mattered* (London: Vintage).

Sterling, S. (2012) *The Future Fit Framework: An Introductory Guide to Teaching & Learning for Sustainability in H.E.* (Plymouth, UK: Plymouth University for the Higher Education Academy).

UN PRME website: http://www.unprme.org/

Visser, M. (2010) *The Quest for Sustainable Business* (Sheffield, UK: Greenleaf Publishing).

Vonnegut, K. (1992) *Player Piano* (London: Flamingo).

22 Giving life to stakeholder theory: A virtual island approach to responsible management education

Roz Sunley

Winchester Business School

University of Winchester, Winchester, England

Introduction

Responsible Management has been a core module in undergraduate and postgraduate study at the Winchester Business School since 2010, reflecting a mission to develop responsible leaders who appreciate their moral and ethical responsibilities, including awareness of the need to generate sustainable value for business and society at large.

This case study illustrates the impact of an innovative teaching approach that was shortlisted for the 'Best Delivered Module of the Year' award in the Winchester University's Student Led Teaching Awards 2013/14. Rather than relying on an intellectual framework of conceptual knowledge and understanding as the basis for responsible management education, first-year business students engage with their own *living experience* of learning as stakeholders in the social, economic and environmental life of a virtual island that uses an open source blogging platform.

Challenge

Responsible Management is a 12-week, first-semester, first-year module. Despite the seeming success of interactive lectures and seminars in the initial teaching of this subject, first-year students sometimes struggle with the breadth and diversity of a module that encompasses corporate responsibility, sustainable development, personal and professional values, and which includes the nature of capitalism and the changing role of business in society. This complexity of topics is the key issue addressed in the module as it tries to reflect the multifaceted challenge of responsible decision-making in contemporary global business. It became apparent that in order to help students deal with the confusion of stakeholder perspectives, what was needed was a context that could reflect real world events, but at the same time actively involve students in the challenging subject matter. Given growing interest in digital scholarship, a virtual island using an open source blogging tool seemed to offer a useful learning platform that students could access on a variety of mobile devices, both inside and outside the classroom. This innovative resource was created by an IT non-specialist, and at no financial cost.

What we did

The creation of a fictional island called Laputare provided an imaginative and interactive panorama in which to engage students in changing social, economic and environmental issues. The building and opening of a new luxury hotel on a small island of outstanding natural beauty, renowned for its flora, fauna and ancient fishing grounds, creates a central narrative that challenges students to raise questions about sustainable business, ethical decision-making, and the type of society they are prepared to support. The fictional island stories offer windows onto real contemporary global events such as an oil spill that is linked to BP's Deepwater Horizon disaster, discussion of offshore wind turbines and controversy over fracking. Current global stories are connected via web links that are regularly revised and updated to ensure relevance each academic year. To maximise student engagement, events on the island are also reported in a light-hearted, celebrity magazine format called Laputare Life that supplements weekly unfolding business storylines.

Students are assigned to one of seven stakeholder groups that represent different interests on the island (local business community, hotel group, island preservation society, etc.) and they are required to engage in collaborative discussion/blogs/presentations about events that unfold via prescheduled weekly newsfeeds. They are also required to vote in elections that can change the axis of power in the island government, decide on proposals to develop sustainable tourism and agree the introduction of a music festival. All these help to illustrate the multi-disciplinary nature of responsible management. Laputare is used alongside weekly lectures, which provide the underpinning theory for the module, but this flexible learning resource forms the basis for all classroom activities and assessments.

What happened

This adaptive social learning space is now in its third year, and student feedback continues to demonstrate the benefits of this interactive approach which encourages students to engage with their own *living experience* of learning as stakeholders, rather than relying on the *lived experience* of corporate strangers in more traditional case studies. Students are challenged to reflect on their own values and personal social responsibility, in parallel with possibly contradictory views held within their particular stakeholder group. They are better prepared to understand the complexities of responsible decision-making after personally experiencing the problems of gaining agreement, not only within their own stakeholder group, but also as an island community where different groups have conflicting interests. The island not only offers opportunities to explore the plurality of values and moral reasoning, but also provides good preparation for the future challenge of 'doing the right thing' in the world of work with its potential conflict between personal and corporate values.

The majority of first-year students agree that the island approach to responsible management is both enjoyable and useful as a learning resource. Comments suggest the island makes course material more immediately relevant as it is a 'great way of understanding the stakeholder model', and 'really helped me apply the material from reading' and because they begin to 'own' evolving events as stakeholders, it also offers 'a really good way of encouraging us to be mindful of world events that we would otherwise not be interested in'; while others comment that it is 'an excellent way of doing assessments and learning'. Even those who do not necessarily like the web-based platform—'I'm not keen on Laputare'—agree 'it is fairly interesting and engaging and different to other modules' or 'Not really a fan of it' but 'understand it from a stakeholder view now'.

One of the potential barriers to operational success has been identified as a lack of engagement by a few academic staff who do not fully understand the narrative or simple navigation of the site. This will become an important area for staff development as colleagues from law, marketing and event management enquire about the potential for their subject discipline to be included in the island. The use of this resource has already been extended to synthesise learning across two first-year business modules.

What next?

Two students, who previously completed the module, have been further developing the island as part of a project to ensure its continuing relevance to new cohorts of students. Biographies of island characters have been written, and additional storylines introduced.

In order to keep this learning resource as up to date as possible for increasingly 'tech-savvy' students, short video films are being included to further stimulate interest in life on the island. These will feature a mixture of local business people and drama students taking on the role of key stakeholders and discussing controversial issues.

Laputare will need to keep evolving if it is to maintain its student reputation as a valuable learning experience, and illustrates our continuing commitment to the Principles for Responsible Management Education.

23 *Developing critical perspectives through case-oriented exercises*

Sachiko Takeda and Davide Secchi

The Business School, Bournemouth University

Bournemouth, England

Introduction

The Business School at Bournemouth University signed up to the Principles for Responsible Management Education (PRME) in 2009. The PRME principles play an important role in the School's endeavour to prepare students as the next generation of business leaders who recognise the importance of ethical and responsible management when confronted with the complex challenges of contemporary business. The PRME principles provide a guiding pointer for our teaching, research and partnership/networking activities. In teaching, we are led by the purpose of developing the capabilities of students and incorporate the values of social responsibility into our academic activities and curriculum. For example, every year we welcome around 250 undergraduate management students. All these students take a management ethics module in the first year, and nearly half of them further their understanding of global sustainability by taking the module of environmental sustainability in their second year. In their final year, a module on corporate social responsibility (CSR) is taken by all students before they graduate. These modules are led by the PRME principle of designing effective learning experiences.

Challenge

Whereas we are given opportunities to provide responsible management education to our undergraduate students through the
three-year programme, postgraduate education poses a different,
more challenging framework. Every year, 200–250 students enrol
on the MSc business management and marketing courses of the
Business School. The majority of them are international students,
many from Asian countries such as China, Thailand and Taiwan.
Most of these students studied in their home countries up to
undergraduate level and had never studied ethics-related topics
before. We therefore face the difficult task of engaging them in
the discourse of social responsibility and ethics within the framework of the one-year programme. A further challenge is posed
by the different teaching methods and approaches taken in their
home countries. As a consequence, many of them find critical
thinking difficult to grasp and find it challenging to use analytical
approaches and applied analyses. The lack of emphasis on ethical
elements in previous studies has been addressed by introducing
CSR concepts, models and theories, and responsible management
in different modules. However, this solution does not trigger the
development of application skills. More importantly, this approach
fails to address the critical and diversified thinking necessary for
the internalisation of ethics-related values.

What we did

Addressing the challenge outlined above, one of the School academics developed case-study-oriented coursework for a module
focused on social responsibility and ethics. A coursework pack
was prepared for use in a two-hour seminar held every week for
10 weeks. The size of the classes, limited to about 20 students
per seminar, permitted a student-centred, discussion-oriented
approach. The course pack consists of 10 exercises (43 pages),

most of which were developed by the course tutor. It is designed to walk students through the following steps: (1) forming their own understanding of social responsibility with their own definitions; (2) applying CSR models, theories and approaches to cases; (3) developing critical abilities; (4) analysing a company using a CSR-related theory; (5) understanding different perspectives involved in a case; and (6) undertaking more comprehensive analyses of different case studies. The contents outline for each week's exercise is:

- *Exercise 1: What is social responsibility?* Students are asked to list five words they associate with the expression 'social responsibility' and write their own definitions using these words. After the class discussion, they revise their definitions and compare them with the academic literature (e.g. Secchi 2007).

- *Exercise 2: Application of a model to a case.* Students read a short article on a CSR model (Carroll 1979), watch a video clip on how safety belts were introduced at Ford Motor Company, and frame the information using the model.

- *Exercise 3: Thinking critically.* Students are encouraged to research and find critiques of Carroll's model, discuss it with other students, and elaborate their own critique. They are then asked to revisit their definitions of CSR.

- *Exercise 4: Application of a theory to a case.* This exercise is based on Mitchell, Agle and Wood's (1997) paper. Students are instructed to find an organisation they would like to analyse and list its stakeholders. They then analyse the stakeholders according to their salience using the framework provided by Mitchell *et al.* (1997).

- *Exercise 5: Ethical dilemma.* Students watch a video of a case, and an ethical dilemma is prompted. They are asked to identify different sides involved in the case. They are then instructed to take one side at a time, analyse the situation from a specific perspective following the provided steps and suggest possible solutions for the respective party. They repeat the process for each side involved in the case.

- *Exercises 6-10: Case studies*. Students read articles, reports and summaries of cases, watch videos (when available) related to social responsibility and responsible management, and carry out comprehensive analyses, using different analytical frameworks. The exercises include analysing the causes of the problems and considering different solutions. Students are encouraged to consider different parties' perspectives and also think from strategic/corporate governance points of view.

What happened

Most of the students who took part in the module commented that they appreciated the case-oriented approach and that the exercises in the course pack were very useful. Some described the experience as something that 'made me think about things I had never considered before' and that encouraged 'in-depth thinking'. At the same time, students found the following points especially challenging. Firstly, most students were not used to applying concepts, models and theories to real cases. For them, theoretical frameworks were far removed from the real world. They consequently found it difficult to connect models and theories with the cases and carry out the applied analyses. Secondly, as many students came from countries where there was strong state control over enterprises, some were not used to questioning the conduct of companies. They also found political dimensions of organisations difficult to grasp. Thirdly, many students lacked critical thinking skills. This was a fundamental issue that we understood to derive at least partly from the nature of educational emphasis in their previous studies. For instance, they were not used to criticising theories and struggled with the third exercise, which asked them to find multiple critiques of a CSR model. Most of the groups managed to find only one critique, and they were surprised to see the existence of a multiple number of critiques, criticising the model from various angles, when critiques from different groups were put together in the class.

In learning responsible management, it is crucial to be able to question the current situation and analyse it from different perspectives. This was what the exercises ultimately aimed to achieve—to help students become able to critically analyse the situation from different perspectives. A student felt the module to be 'essential for the managers of the future' and stated that it helped 'to see and understand different perspectives of managers and corporate strategies'. In fact, many students commented that, though they found it difficult, this—i.e. critical thinking and analysing from multiple perspectives—was what they learned through the exercises. The particular design of this course helped students engage in CSR-related topics and applied analyses, and elicited critical thinking with diverse perspectives.

What next?

In the short term, we aim/plan to further develop the pack. Hoping to select topics/cases that are closer to students' experiences and interests, we have put out a call encouraging students to submit their own exercises/cases. We plan on including the best cases in the pack. We also plan to include role-play exercises. Being able to analyse an issue from different angles allows one to acquire more comprehensive understanding of the problem. Such skills, we believe, are indispensable to responsible management. However, this is a challenge to some students, especially those from different educational backgrounds. In order to address this issue, we plan to let students represent different sides involved in a situation in role-play exercises and emphasise the existence of different perspectives involved in issues. For the longer, medium term, we aim to develop teaching notes on the exercises in the course pack.

We wish to share what we learned through the development and use of the exercises with others within and outside our institution.

References

Carroll, A.B. (1979) 'A Three Dimensional Conceptual Model of Corporate Social Performance', *Academy of Management Review* 4: 497-505.

Michell, R.K., B.R. Agle and D.J. Wood (1997) 'Toward a Theory of Stakeholder Identification and Salience: Defining the Principle of Who and What Really Counts', *Academy of Management Review* 22.4: 853-86.

Secchi, D. (2007) 'Utilitarian, Managerial, and Relational Theories of Corporate Social Responsibility', *International Journal of Management Reviews* 9.4: 347-73.

Appendices

Appendix 1: The Six Principles of the Principles for Responsible Management Education

As institutions of higher education involved in the development of current and future managers we declare our willingness to progress in the implementation, within our institution, of the following Principles, starting with those that are more relevant to our capacities and mission. We will report on progress to all our stakeholders and exchange effective practices related to these principles with other academic institutions:

Principle 1

Purpose: We will develop the capabilities of students to be future generators of sustainable value for business and society at large and to work for an inclusive and sustainable global economy.

Principle 2

Values: We will incorporate into our academic activities and curricula the values of global social responsibility as portrayed in international initiatives such as the United Nations Global Compact.

Principle 3

Method: We will create educational frameworks, materials, processes and environments that enable effective learning experiences for responsible leadership.

Principle 4

Research: We will engage in conceptual and empirical research that advances our understanding about the role, dynamics, and impact of corporations in the creation of sustainable social, environmental and economic value.

Principle 5

Partnership: We will interact with managers of business corporations to extend our knowledge of their challenges in meeting social and environmental responsibilities and to explore jointly effective approaches to meeting these challenges.

Principle 6

Dialogue: We will facilitate and support dialogue and debate among educators, students, business, government, consumers, media, civil society organisations and other interested groups and stakeholders on critical issues related to global social responsibility and sustainability.

We understand that our own organisational practices should serve as an example of the values and attitudes we convey to our students.

Appendix 2: The Ten Principles of the United Nations Global Compact

The United Nations Global Compact's Ten Principles in the areas of human rights, labour, the environment, and anti-corruption enjoy universal consensus and are derived from:

- The Universal Declaration of Human Rights
- The International Labour Organization's Declaration on Fundamental Principles and Rights at Work
- The Rio Declaration on Environment and Development
- The United Nations Convention Against Corruption

The UN Global Compact asks companies to embrace, support, and enact, within their sphere of influence, a set of core values in the areas of human rights, labour standards, the environment, and anti-corruption:

Human Rights

- Principle 1: Businesses should support and respect the protection of internationally proclaimed human rights; and
- Principle 2: make sure that they are not complicit in human rights abuses.

Labour

- Principle 3: Businesses should uphold the freedom of association and the effective recognition of the right to collective bargaining;
- Principle 4: the elimination of all forms of forced and compulsory labour;
- Principle 5: the effective abolition of child labour; and
- Principle 6: the elimination of discrimination in respect of employment and occupation.

Environment

- Principle 7: Businesses should support a precautionary approach to environmental challenges;
- Principle 8: undertake initiatives to promote greater environmental responsibility; and
- Principle 9: encourage the development and diffusion of environmentally friendly technologies.

Anti-Corruption

- Principle 10: Businesses should work against corruption in all its forms, including extortion and bribery.

Appendix 3:
Co-editor biographies

Professor Alan Murray holds the Hoare Chair in Responsible Management at Winchester Business School, where he is Head of Research and Knowledge Exchange, in the Faculty of Business, Law and Sport. Alan has been closely connected to the PRME initiative right from the beginning having been part of the original UN Global Compact Taskforce which developed the Principles in 2006/7. In 2006, he also instigated the establishment of the British Academy of Management Special Interest Group in Corporate Social Responsibility (now renamed as the Sustainable and Responsible Management SIG), and became its founding Chair. In subsequent years he ran, with colleagues in what is now the UK and Ireland regional Chapter, a succession of events both to promote PRME and also to offer support in the teaching and researching of subjects con-nected to the wide notion of Responsible Management. Since then, he has published several articles and book chapters within this field, as well as co-authoring, with Michael Blowfield, the first edi-tion of *Corporate Responsibility*, published by Oxford University Press in 2008. A second edition was published in 2011 which won the Chartered Management Institute's 'Management Book of the Year 2011–12'. A third edition is forthcoming.

Alec Wersun is a senior lecturer in strategy and international business in the Glasgow School for Business and Society (GSBS). A member of UNPRME's Advisory Group, and recently elected Co-Chair of the UK Chapter of PRME, Alec leads his own University's efforts to embed PRME in to the fabric of the School's teaching, research and external engagement. GSBS tries to 'walk the talk' of responsible leadership and management through active engagement with the UK's largest corporate responsibility organisation, Business in the Community, and its sister organisation in Scotland, Scottish Business in the Community.

Professor Kathryn Haynes holds the Northern Society Chair in Accounting & Finance at Newcastle University Business School, UK, where she is currently Deputy Director responsible for Research and formerly Head of the Accounting & Finance Subject Group. Kathryn is a Chartered Accountant and Fellow of the Institute of Chartered Accountants in England and Wales (ICAEW). Kathryn is also a Fellow of the Advanced Institute of Management Research (AIM), where she was Lead Fellow of the Services research cohort. She is a co-facilitator of the Gender Equality Working Group of the UN Principles for Responsible Management Education. Kathryn's research broadly relates to issues of social responsibility and the role of accounting in society. She is particularly interested in issues of gender and diversity in relation to education, professions and professional services, addressing identity and its relationship with gender; the body and embodiment within organisations; the juxtaposition of professional and personal identities; and the conduct of the professions and professional services firms. She also works in the area of sustainability, accountability and social responsibility, and is currently working on a project linking gender equality and sustainability. Her work has been funded by the ESRC and has been published in leading journals such as *Accounting Organizations & Society*, *Accounting, Auditing and Accountability Journal* and *Gender, Work & Organization*.

Denise Baden (PhD, Soton) followed her first degree in Politics with Economics with several years in industry; she then returned to academia to undertake a doctorate in psychology, which was awarded in 2002. Denise worked in the area of social psychology for 3 years, and then joined the Southampton Management School as a lecturer in 2005, where she has been engaged in research and teaching in the areas of business ethics, sustainability, entrepreneurship and corporate social responsibility.

Paul Cashian is Director of Learning and Teaching for the Faculty of Business, Environment and Society at Coventry University and has responsibility for embedding sustainability within the curriculum across the faculty. Prior to this he spent 7 years as Associate Dean (Student Experience) and 12 years as Head of the Business Subject Group. Originally an economist, Paul's research interests revolve around developing a critical realist approach to the evaluation of management practice.

Appendix 4: Contributor biographies

Dr Denise Baden lectures in Business Ethics and Corporate Social Responsibility at the School of Management, University of Southampton. Her current research interests are sustainability, behaviour change, business ethics, CSR and small business.

Tina Bass is Deputy Head of the Strategy and Applied Management Department at Coventry University Business School

Dr Eshani Beddewela is the Business School representative for the PRME at the University of Huddersfield and is a Lecturer in Corporate Social Responsibility.

Karen Blakeley is Senior Lecturer in Leadership and Management and Director of the Centre for Responsible Management at Winchester Business School.

Dr John Blewitt is Co-Director of the MSc Social Responsibility and Sustainability at Aston Business School, and is author of *Understanding Sustainable Development* (2014, 2nd edn) and *Media Ecology and Conservation* (Green Books, 2010).

Jack Christian is a Senior Lecturer and Faculty PRME champion at Manchester Metropolitan University Business School. He teaches Ethics and Sustainability Accounting with a primary research interest in Biodiversity Accounting.

Catherine Court is the Faculty Manager of Strathclyde Business School, providing senior management support to deliver the overall strategy.

Laura Davidson is the Assistant Faculty Manager at Strathclyde Business School, responsible for the academic quality experience of its students.

Jana Filosof is a principal lecturer in the Strategic Management group, Hertfordshire Business School. She is a Director of Social Enterprise Unit and a PRiME Champion.

Dr Kyoko Fukukawa is a Senior Lecturer in Marketing at Bradford University School of Management and specialises in research on CSR and ethical decision-making in consumption and business practices.

Dr Jane Gibbon is Senior Lecturer in Accounting at Newcastle University Business School, where she specialises in research on social accounting and accountability, and is the School's PRME champion.

Helyn Gould is Vice Dean Academic at Strathclyde Business School and has an interest in innovative learning, particularly involving technology.

Susan Grant coordinates and supports Glasgow Caledonian University's Community and Public Engagement (CPE) Steering Group and is the main point of contact for CPE activity at GCU.

Dr Radi Haloub is a Lecturer in strategy at the University of Huddersfield, member of the Chartered Institute of Marketing (MCIM) and a Chartered Marketer.

Professor Kathryn Haynes holds the Northern Society Chair in Accounting & Finance at Newcastle University Business School where she is Deputy Director of the School, and Head of the Gender, Professions and Society Research Group. She is a Co-facilitator of the PRME Gender Equality Working Group.

John Hirst is Senior Teaching Fellow in Management at Durham University Business School and the Bursar of Ustinov College within Durham University.

Dr Briga Hynes lectures in entrepreneurship at the Kemmy Business School, University of Limerick, and currently serves on the Limerick City Enterprise Board (Board member); Southill Development Cooperative; Chair Mentoring Advisory Group (Paul Partnership) and Access Campus Board (University of Limerick).

Dr Steve Kempster is Professorial Director of Leadership Development, Lancaster Leadership Centre, Lancaster University Management School. Steve's research specialisms include leadership learning, leadership practice, and leadership purpose and ethics.

Dr Sheila Killian is Director of Principles for Responsible Management Education at the Kemmy Business School, University of Limerick, where she also serves as Assistant Dean, Research.

Dr Stephen Kinsella is a Senior Lecturer in Economics at the Kemmy Business School, University of Limerick. He studies the Irish and European economies and has written four books and is a weekly columnist for the *Irish Independent.*

Carly Lamont is lecturer in Organisational Behaviour and Human Resource Management and Peer-Assisted Learning (PAL) coordinator.

Dr John Lever is Lecturer in Sustainability at the University of Huddersfield. John's research and teaching focuses on sustainable food production and consumption with a specific focus on farm animal welfare.

Colm McLaughlin is Senior Lecturer in Industrial Relations and Human Resource Management and PRME Coordinator for the UCD School of Business.

Dr Julia Meaton is Senior Lecturer and course leader for the MSc Risk, Disaster and Environmental Management at the University of Huddersfield. Julia's recent research has focused on refugees and housing sustainability in Jordan.

Dr Walter Mswaka is Senior Lecturer in Business Strategy at the University of Huddersfield. Walter is a business adviser with extensive experience of offering advice and technical support to small- and medium-sized enterprises (SMEs).

Andrea Prothero is Associate Dean for Academic Affairs at the UCD School of Business, and lectures in the marketing subject area.

Davide Secchi currently works in the areas of individual social responsibility and socially based decision-making.

Dr Stephen Simister is an Associate Professor at Henley Business School and combines his academic role at Henley on MBA and leadership programmes, with a consultancy role working for a number of organisations on their change initiatives.

Dr Anne M.J. Smith lectures on entrepreneurship and innovation in the Glasgow School for Business and Society and publishes in international journals in the fields of rural entrepreneurship, learning and enterprise education.

Dr Jean-Anne Stewart is an Associate Professor at Henley Business School and Programme Director for the MA Leadership & Corporate MBA programmes

Dr Roz Sunley teaches responsible management at Winchester Business School and is passionate about creative pedagogy for business management, and engaging students in their own learning.

Nathan Tagg is a Senior Development Officer at Glasgow Caledonian University, and manages the Caledonian Club.

Sachiko Takeda is a Senior Lecturer in Global Corporate Social Responsibility and School representative to PRME.

Dr Julie C. Thomson is a lecturer in the Glasgow School for Business and Society and lectures on business management subjects including entrepreneurship and innovation.

Dr Lynn Thurloway is an Associate Professor at Henley Business School, the Programme Director for the Health and Social Care Management Programme and is the Subject Area Leader for the Management Research Challenge.

Emma Watton is Senior Teaching Fellow, Management Development Division, Lancaster University Management School. Emma's research interests are in the areas of responsible leadership, leadership resilience and leadership reform in the financial services sector.

Dr Alec Wersun is Co-Chair of the Glasgow Caledonian University PRME Leadership Team, senior lecturer in strategy, and a Community and Public Engagement Fellow.

Adrian Wood is Professor of Sustainability at the University of Huddersfield. He has been involved in research, teaching and field activities concerned with African development and the environment for more than three decades.